Letterheads/6

The International Annual of Letterhead Design

David E. Carter
Editor

No design appearing in this book
may be copied without the permission
of the owner of that design.

ISBN: 0-88108-038-1
LCCC#: 78-640636
STANDING ISBN FOR SERIES: 0-910158-41-X

Art Direction Book Co.
10 E. 39th Street
New York, NY 10016

The designs and captions in this book
have been supplied by the designers and/or
firms represented. While every effort has been
made to ensure accuracy, David E. Carter and
Art Direction Book Co., do not, under any
circumstances, accept responsibility for errors
or omissions.

Printed in Hong Kong.

This is the sixth in a series of books showing outstanding letterhead designs from around the world.

If you would like to submit designs for possible inclusion, please follow this procedure:

(1) mail all letterheads unmounted and flat.

(2) send your entries to *Art Direction Book Company, 10 East 39th Street, New York, New York 10016.*

There is no entry or hanging fee of any kind.

The editor wishes to express his thanks to Wanda Greer who worked many hours to make sure this book was completed by the deadline.

And, once again, a special word of appreciation to my daughters, Christa and Lauren, who look forward to helping their dad work on each volume of this book.

Letterheads & Designers

1983 Breakers Sales Rally . . . .
24 Carrot. . . . . .Walter R. McCord
A House For All Seasons. . . . . .Sandy Blake
Acare. . . . . Simons Group
Actus Dance Institute . . . .
Adam James . . . . Cheryl Lewin
Airtel Plaza Stationery . . . . Bill Taylor;. . . . .
. . . . Taylor & Wilson
Alan Niilo . . . . .Alan Niilo
Alan's Bake Shop . . . . The Art House
Albin Upp. Bruno Oldani
Amy Friedman, Writer . . . . Linda Benveniste
Andrea Sachse. . . . . .Marjorie Krasnick
Angelo Vecchione. . . . . Rinaldo Cutini
Antonello Tiracchia. . . . . Rinaldo Cutini
Architectural Book Center . . . . .Young & Martin
. . . . Design
Art Directors Club of New Jersey . . . . . .Roger Dowd
Art West . . . . Michael Blair; DYR—Art West
Arthurs, Biedrycki & Associates, Inc. . . . .
. . . . .Sam N. Morgan
Artocean Aquarium Engineering Ltd. . . . .The Group
. . . . .Advertising Ltd.
Arturo Di Boote . . . . Rinaldo Cutini
Ayesha Soni, Photographer . . . . Urshila Kerkar
Balans As. . . . . Bruno Oldani
Ballet Coppelia . . . . Oswaldo Miranda
Basys Inc. . . . . .Robert Cooney
Bay East Graphics. . . . . Bay East Graphics
Beaver Creek Properties. . . . . .Jim Wise
Bellagraf . . . . Rinaldo Cutini
Bi Design. Bi Design
Bill Robinson . . . . Martha Voutas Productions
Bob Calmer Photography . . . .
Bonsai Israel Ltd. . . . . .Michael Levin
Breadline Catering NYC . . . . .Barry Zaid Graphic
. . . . Design
Brumunddal Fro . . . . Bruno Oldani
Burdett Optical Company . . . . . . .Peter Kerr Design
Calligrafia . . . . Oswaldo Miranda
Camping Ca' Pasquali . . . . .Diorgio Davanzo
Cape La Jolla. . . . . .Ted Hansen Design
Carlos Grasseti. . . . . Oswaldo Miranda
Carmichael's . . . . .Walter R. McCord
Carrozzeria Jesolana . . . . .Giorgio Davanzo
Cary Staples . . . . .Cary Staples
Casa. . . . . .Ian Price
Cash Lewman Real Estate . . . . . . .Walter R. McCord

CBS Merchandising Program . . . . .Nancy Hoefiz
CBS Records . . . . Christopher Austopchuk
Cellular One . . . . . Jack Anderson; Hornall Anderson
. . . . Design
Centre Dentaire Duquet . . . . Pierre Drovin
Chaffey Corp. Baseball Club . . . . . . .Warren Wilkin &
. . . . .Tommer Peterson
Child Nutrition Program . . . . . Adwest Graphics, Inc.
Claudio Carvalho. . . . . Claudio Carvalho
Claus F. Weidmuller . . . . .Claus F. Weidmuller
Clausen Advertising. . . . . Clausen Advertising
Clayers . . . . Bob Costanza
Coins. Oswaldo Miranda
Colorband USA. . . . . Tim Hanlon
Columbia Albums . . . . .Allen Weinberg
Commerce Park. . . . .
Commercial Lithographing Co. . . . .
. . . . .Juan Lopez-Bonilla
Commonwealth. . . . . Peter Birren
Compu-Mark-U.S. . . . . .Victoria Martin;
. . . . Sparkman/Bartholomew Associates
Construtora. . . . . Oz Comunicacao Grafica
Coombs Consulting Ltd. . . . . .Robynne Ranft;
. . . . .The Ranft Plan
Cypher + Nichols + Design . . . . . . Raymond Nichols;
. . . . .Cypher + Nichols + Design
Danica Meglic . . . . Studio Krog
Datamation Services, Inc. . . . . Bob Daniels
Design & Type. . . . . .Tony Agpoon
Design In Action . . . . Design In Action
Design International . . . . .Tim Girvin Design Inc.
Diane Moon Graphics . . . . Diane Moon
Dianne Parker & Associates, Inc.. . . . .
. . . . .Beery Associates, Inc.
Discos & Producoes Artisticas Ltda. . . . . . . .Claudio
. . . . .Carvalho
Dix Ans. . . . . Legault Nolin Larosee
Doge Gritti . . . . .Giorgio Davanzo
Don Wilson Construction Co., Ltd. . . . . Graphic
. . . . .Design Systems
Doppler. . . . . Young & Martin Design
Douglas Development Co. . . . . Mark E. Lewis
Dr. Jay Jacobson. . . . . Julian Navarro &
. . . . .Brenda Bodney
E.T. Cronin Designs. . . . . .B.C. Graphics
Eagle Pacific Insurance Company . . . .Jack Anderson;
. . . . Hornall Anderson Design
Earth Conversions Inc. . . . . Abraham J. Amuny

Elaine Pantages . . . . .Elaine Pantages
Elka. . . . . Oz Comunicacao Grafica
Enterac . . . . Legault Nolin Larosee
Entertainment Marketing Concepts. . . .Carol Banever
Exotic Paradise . . . . Eve Creations
Eytan Kaufman. . . . . .Beery Associates, Inc.
Falcon. . . . . .Bruce Benke
Fellowship Baptist Church . . . . .Graphic Design
. . . . Systems
Festival International . . . . Rinaldo Cutini
Fiberforms . . . . Belinda Von Feldt
Flowers From Holland . . . . .Brad Copeland;
. . . . .Cooper Copeland Inc.
Fook Tak Temple . . . . .Designers Express
For Kids Only . . . . Janice M. Lobbins
Forino Jones Design Venture . . .June Robinson-Nall;
. . . . .Martha Vouras Productions Inc.
Forsythe-French-Inc.. . . . . .Norman P. Stromdahl
Four Stars National Golf Tournament. . . . . Jim Allen
. . . . .Design Team
Franc Ambroz. . . . . Studio Krog
Frances Lee Jasper . . . . .Walter R. McCord
Franklin Mushroom Farms . . . .
Freddie Reding, Writer . . . . .Rick Korge
Glade Swimming Pools Ltd. . . . . .Davids Design
Global Tracing Services. . . . . .Bill Bhilipovich
Goldmazon .Marc Iso
Government Service Insurance System . . . .
. . . . Mark E. Lewis
Grafica . . . . Oswaldo Miranda
Graham Catlin + Associates. . . . .
Graphic Design Systems . . . .Graphic Design Systems
Graphic Ink. . . . . Graphic Ink
Graphics One. . . . . Graphics One
Greg Newman . . . . .Sandra Holt, Designer
Groupthink. . . . . The Adams Group
Guti Producoes . . . . Claudio Carvalho
HBO/Cinemax. . . . . .George Pierson/Etta Siegel
Richard Hatch, Magician . . . . Karen Kleinerman
Healthstyles. . . . . .Burson-Marsteller
Holly Small . . . . .John Oswald
Hollywood, Kentucky. . . . . Denise Spaulding
Hospital For Sick Children . . . . Joe Shyllit
Hotelnet . . . . Rick Brown
Images. . . . . Images
Independent Pictures. . . . . .John Adams
International Bank Of The Pacific. . . . . Michael Lee
Irene Borger . . . . .Susan Mayer
Ivy International Inc. . . . . .Sales By Design/
. . . . .The Martin Agency
Jack Davis Graphics. . . . . .Jack W. Davis
Jack Stone Graphic Design . . . . Jack Stone
Jackie Shroft. . . . . Urshila Kerkar
Jan Rieckhoff . . . . Juergen Rieckhoff
Jean L. Brady . . . . .Jean L. Brady
Jeffery A. Yip . . . . Jeffery A. Yip

Jim Laser, Photographer . . . . .Jack Anderson;
. . . . Hornall Anderson Design
John Ayriss .Davis Ayriss
John Hornall Design Works . . . . . . .Jack R. Anderson
John Leffler Music Inc. . . . . R. Anthony Russo
John Sposato. . . . . John Sposato
John Hopkins Medical Institution . . . . . . Janet Nebel;
. . . . The Woods Group, Inc.
Jose Luis Ortiz . . . . .Jose Luis Ortiz
Joseph Feigenbaum. . . . . Joseph Feigenbaum
June Haywood . . . . . . .Wayne Pederson; Seay Design
. . . . .Office
Jungle Jim's. Tim Girvin
K.C.C.O. . . . . Urshila Kerkar
Karel Lamut . . . . Studio Krog
Kavita Sahni . . . . Urshila Kerkar
Ken Cato. . . . . Ken Cato
Kristi Johnson Simkins . . . . . .Kristi Johnson Simkins
Lawrence Ross Publishing . . . .
Lely Palms Of Naples . . . . The Adams Group
Lemons Communications . . . . Bob Mynster;
. . . . .Studiographix
Len Wayne Creative Services . . . . Bi Design
Lifespring . . . . . . Ark Stein; The Blank Design Group
Lindemans Legat. . . . . Bruno Oldani
Lynnhaven . . . . Louis Nelson
M. Caren Connolly . . . .
M. Petek Properties . . . .
Management . . . . .Carol Baneuer
Marchman. . . . . .Patt Farrell; Crackerjack Studio
Mark Lewis Design . . . . .Mark Lewis Design
Market Design . . . . Market Design
Matthew Klein Studio . . . .
MCI Communications . . . .
Mercedes Lemos Gameiro . . . . .Oswaldo Miranda
Miami Children's Hospital . . . . . Advertising & Design
Michael Badger . . . . . . Richard Foy; Communication
. . . . .Arts Inc.
Mickey Mantle/Whitey Ford Fantasy Baseball Camp. .
. . . . .Wanda Greer/Denise Spaulding
Mike Berne .Mike Berne
Mike Condon, Inc.. . . . . Mike Condon
Mike Hodges . . . . .Mike Hodges
Myrna Davis . . . . .Paul Davis
Nancy Stevenson. . . . .
National Ballet Of Canada. . . . . . Parsons Associates
National Child Watch Campaign . . . . . . Hien Nguyen
National Self-Helf Center . . . . Simons Group
Native Tree . . . . Young & Martin Design
Ned Culic Design. . . . . Ned Culic Design
Neon Studio . . . . .Felipe Taborda
New Richmond Supply Laundries. . . . . . Tim Girvin
. . . . Design, Inc.
Nireu Jose Telxelra . . . . .Oswaldo Miranda
Ohio Printing Co. . . . . .Ruth Leonard; Salvato & Coe
. . . . .Associates

One Service . . . . Claudio Carvalho
Orcoll Business Services. . . . . Robert Casey
Orion Metals . . . Ray Wandling; R. Falk Design Group
Oswaldo Miranda. . . . . Oswaldo Miranda
Our Lady Of The Lake Fountain. . . . . Chuck Nivens;
. . . . Anna Macedo & Company
Owens/Lutter . . . . Christine Owens
Oz Communicacao Grafica . . . . . . Oz Communicacao
. . . . Grafica
Paradiso. . . . . Arturoui
Parsons Associates. . . . . Parsons Associates
Party Factory . . . . Mark Wasserman
Patricia Ryan Schmidt. . . . . Michael M. Smit
Paul Davis Studios. . . . . Paul Davis
Paul Pullara Graphic Design. . . . . Paul Pullara
Pearce . . . . Peter Kerr Design
Pedro Ho Photography . . . .
Penguin Recording . . . . David Ayriss Design
People Magazine . . . . . . .Arthur Beckstein; Time Inc.
Peter Kerr Design Associates . . . . . Peter Kerr Design
. . . . Associates
Peter Levenson, Architect . . . . Leslie Kameny
Peter Ravn Design. . . . . Peter Ravn
Piper Trust . . . . .Jim Allen Design Team
Portalandre Sala . . . .
Portland Museum . . . . .Walter R. McCord
Poty Lazzarotto . . . . Oswaldo Miranda
Powder Mountain Resorts . . . . .See Level Design
Prairie Lands Classic . . . . Jack W. Davis
Private Showing. . . . . .Dalia Hartman, Designer
Pro Packaging . . . . Bi Design
Provident Companies. . . . . Jon Cornwell
Psychiatric Diagnostic Labs Of America . . . .
. . . . Rosa Farber; Kallir, Phillips, Ross
Quixote. . . . . Oswaldo Miranda
Radio Sole 104.6. . . . . .Arturoui
Rainbow Real Estate. . . . . Robert Midura
Rick Swayer . . . . Reagan Dunnick; Houston
Rinaldo Cutini. . . . . Rinaldo Cutini
Riverparc. . . . .
Robert K. Miller . . . . .Synthesis Concepts, Inc.
Robert Minuzzo . . . . William D. Gibbs
Rogersrough Layout . . . . .Ronny Shinder
Roslyn Veterinary Group . . . . Bob Costanza
Rowland + Eleanor Bingham Miller. . . . .
. . . . .Walter R. McCord
Saiki & Associates. . . . . Saiki & Associates
Sam. . . . . Bruno Aldani
Sandoval . . . .
Scott H. Osborne Design . . . . Scott H. Osborne
Seabank. . . . . .Crackerjack Studio
Serano Vianello. . . . . .Giorgio Davanzo
Sesame . . . . .Dan Reisinger
Shot In The Dark Studios . . . . Michael Orr
Signos . . . . Oswaldo Miranda
Site Research Group . . . . .Walter R. McCord

Southern Health Services. . . . . .Susan Martz;
. . . . Sparkman/Bartholomew Associates
Specialty Direct Marketing . . . . Marion Seay;
. . . . Seay Design Office
Spectrum Photo Labs . . . . .Michael M. Smit
Squash Inn .Atruroui
St. James Court. . . . . Urshila Kerkar
Stuart Fink . . . . Vahe Fattal
Summer At The Centre . . . . Parsons Associates
Summerfield Graphics. . . . .
TSI Communications. . . . . Frank Benintendo
Tania Energy Inc. . . . . Jerry Cowart
The Agency. . . . . Urshila Kerkar
The Blue & The Gray . . . .
The Bridgeway . . . . .Louis Nelson Associates
The Catalogue Group . . . . Barbara Borejko
The Children's Aid Society . . . . . Parsons Associates
The Eye. . . . . Jin Wise
The Framemaker. . . . . .Steve St. John;
. . . . .D' Acosta Advertising
The Group Advertising Ltd. . . . . The Group
. . . . Advertising Ltd.
The Judge . . . . Jerry Cowart
The Paper Company . . . . Bi Design
The Quorum . . . . .Vitale & Associates
The Seidman Company . . . . .Michael M. Smit
The Sports Club/LA . . . . Cozad & Associates
The Woods Group . . . . .Janet Nebel; The Woods
. . . . Group Inc.
Thomas Hillman Design.. . . . . .Thomas Hillman
Thomsen Dental Associates. . . . .
Tish McCutchen . . . . Suzanne Anderson
Toni Holzel Grafik Design. . . . . Toni Holzel
Tony Paris Associates, Inc. . . . . Tony Paris
Travel Associates. . . . . .Karen Fults Kaler
Triloka Trading Company . . . . .Phillip Tang;
. . . . .The Woods Group Inc.
Ultron Corp. . . . . .Mary Bogdan/Sol Lang
UMI Design . . . . Yumi Tanimoto
University Of Iowa . . . . Mark E. Lewis
Uwe Schmidt. . . . . .Ubi Muziek
Virginia Institute Of Marine Science . . Mark E. Lewis
Vision Gallery, Inc. . . . . Primo Angeli Graphics
Vitale & Associates . . . . .Vitale & Associates
Von Feldt Design . . . . Belinda Von Feldt
Warkulwiz Design Associates. . . . . .Warkulwiz Design
. . . . .Associates
Way Out West Graphic Design. . . . . . Jerry Tokugawa
Wayne Pederson . . . . . .Wayne Pederson; Seay Design
. . . . .Office
Weatherford . . . . . . .Robert Wolf; Landor Associates
Wendy Griffith . . . . .Wendy Griffith
Widewaters Group. . . . . . . Stetson Turner Associates
Wilfried Wolter, Fotograf . . . . .Richard Muller
Wilson & Wilson . . . . .Wilson & Wilson
WQEZ 99 . . . . .Advertising Center Inc.
Xavier-Feal . . . . .Xavier-Feal
Zirkle Lee & Associates. . . . . Carole Nergiv

The designs appearing in this book have been
submitted by either the designer or the client,
for use in this publication. Further reproduction
is prohibited.

JOHN SPOSATO
Illustration & Design · 43 E. 22 St., NYC, 10010 · (212) 477-3909

JOHN SPOSATO
Illustration & Design
43 E. 22 St., NYC, 10010

JOHN SPOSATO · Illustration & Design · 43 E. 22 St., NYC, 10010 · (212) 477-3909

T

TSI
COMMUNICATIONS
SIXTEEN WEST
FORTY-SIXTH
STREET

S

NEW YORK
10036
NEW YORK
(212)
869-8787

I

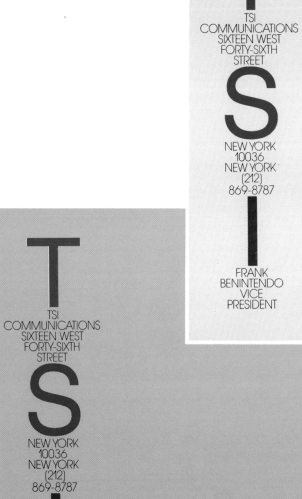

T

TSI
COMMUNICATIONS
SIXTEEN WEST
FORTY-SIXTH
STREET

S

NEW YORK
10036
NEW YORK
(212)
869-8787

I

FRANK
BENINTENDO
VICE
PRESIDENT

T

TSI
COMMUNICATIONS
SIXTEEN WEST
FORTY-SIXTH
STREET

S

NEW YORK
10036
NEW YORK
(212)
869-8787

I

ART·WEST

4751 Wilshire Boulevard
Suite 201
Los Angeles CA 90010
(213) 930-5000

ART·WEST

4751 Wilshire Boulevard
Suite 201
Los Angeles CA 90010
(213) 930-5000

Bonsai Israel Ltd.
Moshav Bnei-Zion
Israel 60910
Tel. 052-441596

בונסאי ישראל בע"מ
מושב בני ציון 60910
טל. 052‎‏441596

Bonsai Israel Ltd.
Moshav Bnei-Zion
Israel 60910
Tel. 052-441596

בונסאי ישראל בע"מ
מושב בני ציון 60910
טל. 052‎‏441596

TONI HÖLZL

GRAFIK DESIGN

PROGETTAZIONE GRAFICA
ANDRIAN - ANDRIANO (BZ)
BINDERGASSE 2 VIA DEI BOTTAI
TEL. (0471) 57234

HANDELSKAMMER / C.C.I.A.A. BZ 103031

MWST. / P. IVA 00684410210 - RAIKA ANDRIAN / CASSA RURALE DI ANDRIANO C/C 20248/7 -

Elka Plásticos Ltda
Avenida Casa Verde 472
Parque Peruche São Paulo SP
CEP 02520 PBX (011)290·6288
Telex (011)36.724 ELKA BR

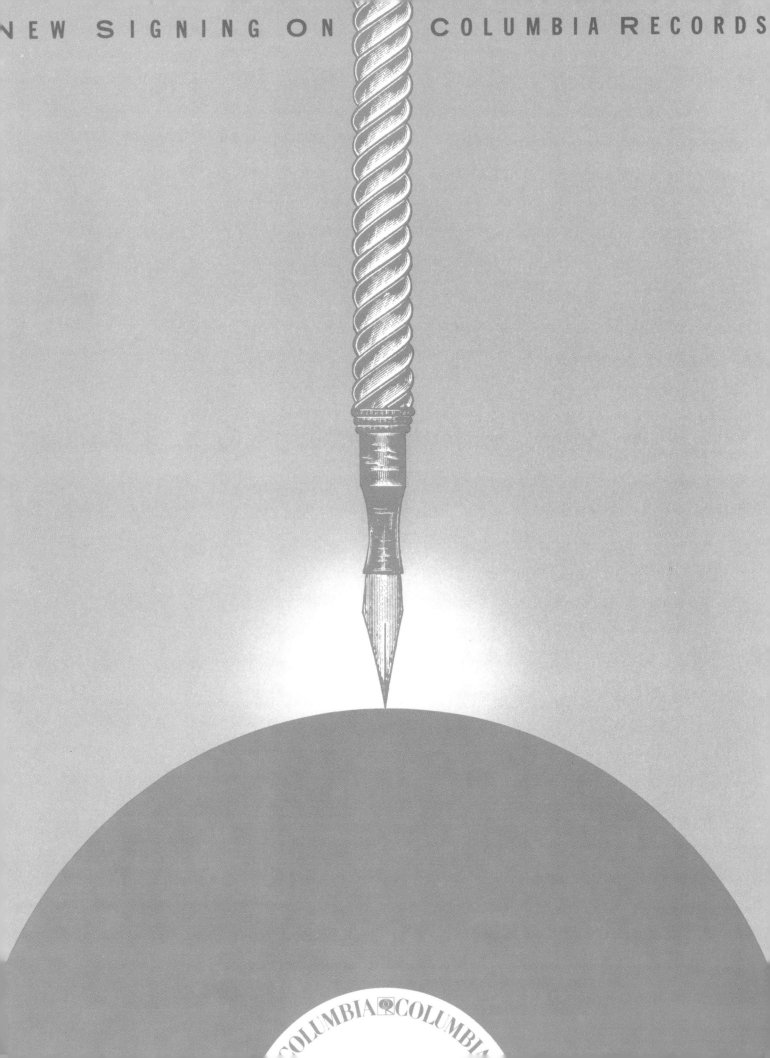

Much of society runs on the fuel of habit. Things happen as they have happened before. Situations arise as they have arisen before. In turn, it seems that each of us has an effect on society that has happened before.

When things run smoothly, it is nice to lie back and feel the warmth of the good life. Ah, the habit of the good life: there is security in predictability.

But this predictability can eat away at innovative and creative thinking.

Creative thinking needs a constructive discontent with the way things were before.

Ah, to do things simply because that's the way they were before.

No, thank you.

Cypher+Nichols+Design
503 Windsor Drive
Newark, Delaware 19711
(302) 454-1411

Cypher+Nichols+Design
503 Windsor Drive
Newark, Delaware 19711
(302) 454-1411

Cypher+Ni...ls+Design
503 Windso...ve
Newark, Del...e 19711
(302) 454-14...

21 Via Plinio 00193 Roma
Telefono 3599595

ANTONELLO TIRACCHIA

THE BLUE  THE GRAY

CBS ENTERTAINMENT, PRESS INFORMATION
51 WEST 52 STREET, NEW YORK, NY 10019

DOPPLER

Doppler
1922 Piedmont
Circle NE
Atlanta, Georgia
30324
404-873-6941

HOLLY SMALL

ON GRANDIT
ENSEMBLE
LES GRANDS FRÈRES
ET GRANDES SOEURS
DE MONTRÉAL
1975-1985

 Les Grands Frères et
Grandes Soeurs de Montréal Inc.
3740, rue Berri, bureau 390
Montréal (Québec) H2L 4G9
Téléphone: (514) 842-9715

il Genio ANTIPATICO

CREATIVITÀ E TECNOLOGIA
DELLA MODA ITALIANA
1951/1983

"ARTURO DI BOOTE" DI RONCORONI PIA SNC/VIA GUIDO BANTI 19/00191 ROMA TEL. (06) 390022/C.F. 05699280581

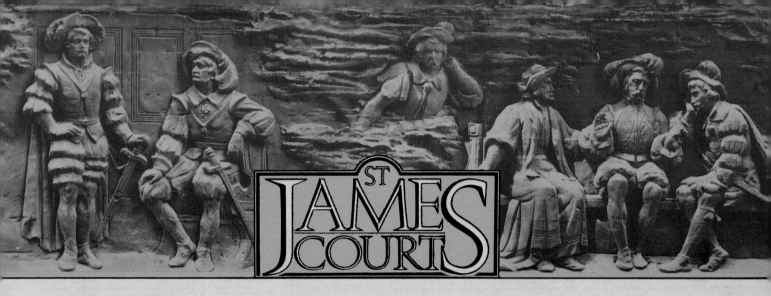

RINALDO CUTINI EDITORE
VIA GIACOMO FAVRETTO 24
00147 ROMA
TELEFONO (06) 5120782

CODICE FISCALE CTN RLD 37T03 H501T
PARTITA IVA 01952810586

spectrum
photo
labs

spectrum
photo
labs

10835 midwest industrial blvd.
st. louis, missouri 63132

10835 midwest industrial blvd.
st. louis, missouri 63132
314-423-8111

Bay East Graphics

171 Eastern Rd. Pasadena, Maryland 21122, 255-5940

Jean L. Brady • 55 Fourth Place • Brooklyn • NY • 11231 • 212 624 3851

Specialty Direct Marketing, Inc.

107 Pennsylvania Avenue
Falls Church, Virginia
22046-3275

703-237-4800

Specialty *Direct Marketing, Inc.*

107 Pennsylvania Avenue
Falls Church, Virginia
22046-3275

he🍎lthstyles

A New Dimension
in Medical Reporting

c/o Burson-Marsteller, 866 Third Avenue, New York, NY 10022

FIBERFORMS

Three Dimensional Fiber Art
Sculptural Tapestry

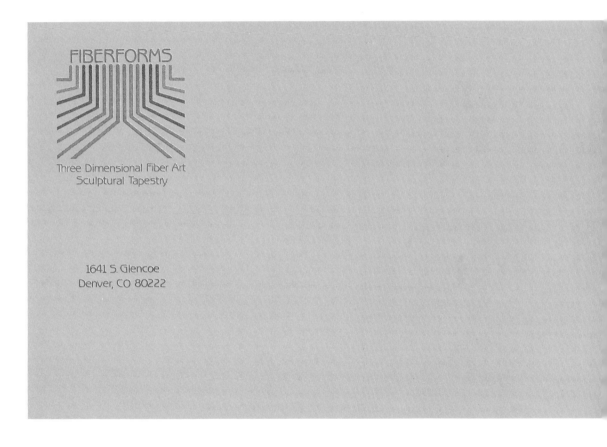

FIBERFORMS

Three Dimensional Fiber Art
Sculptural Tapestry

1641 S. Glencoe
Denver, CO 80222

Sarah Leete
1641 S. Glencoe
Denver, CO 80222

(303) 759-3571

Our Lady of the Lake Foundation

Post Office Box 91160
Baton Rouge, Louisiana 70821

Our Lady of the Lake Foundation

Post Office Box 91160
Baton Rouge, Louisiana 70821

DIANNE PARKER & ASSOC., INC. 137 LODGE AVE., HUNTINGTON, N.Y. 11746   516-423-3250 / N.Y.C. 212-652-1545

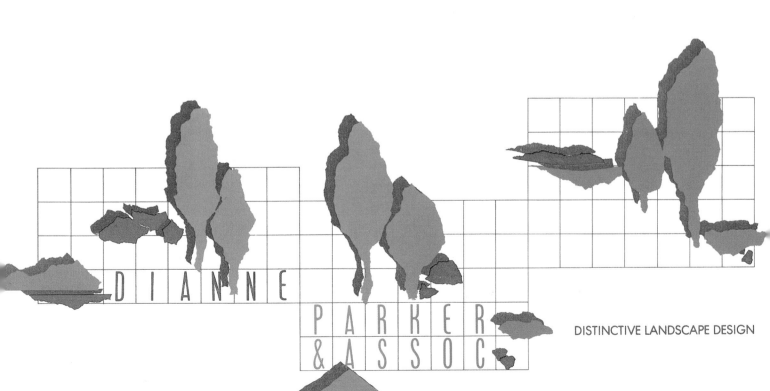

DIANNE PARKER & ASSOC

DISTINCTIVE LANDSCAPE DESIGN

Headquarters
1705 Skyline Tower
10900 N.E. 4th
Bellevue, WA 98004
206.454.4422

bellagraf

THOMAS HILLMAN DESIGN
Advertising/Graphic Design
193 Middle Street
Portland, Maine 04101
207-773-3727

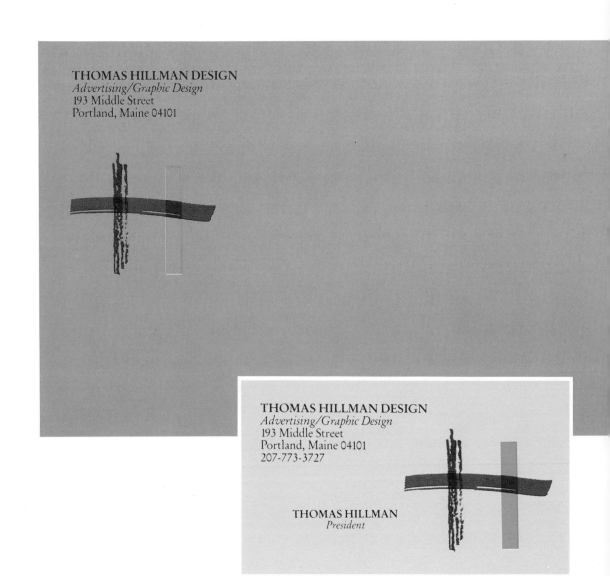

thomsen
dental
associates, p.c.

thomsen
dental
associates, p.c.

4848 so. 120 st.
omaha, ne. 68137

allen l. thomsen, d.d.s.

4848 so. 120 st.
omaha, ne. 68137
phone: 895-3535

FOUR STARS
NATIONAL PRO-CELEBRITY
GOLF TOURNAMENT

140 Brompton Road,
London SW3. England.
Telephone: 01·225 0444
Telex: 919561

TOURNAMENT PROMOTER:
Stars International Golf Limited.
REGISTERED IN ENGLAND:
Number 1841933.
REGISTERED OFFICE:
9 Southampton Row, London WC1B 5HA.

Ned Culic Design
90 Clyde Street St Kilda
Victoria 3182 Australia
Telephone 534 6445

Ned Culic Design
90 Clyde Street St Kilda
Victoria 3182 Australia
Telephone 534 6445

Ned Culic Design
90 Clyde Street St Kilda
Victoria 3182 Australia
Telephone 534 6445

Invoice No

To

Client

Date

Order No

Job No

Ned Culic Design
90 Clyde Street St Kilda
Victoria 3182 Australia
Telephone 534 6445

GRAPHIC DESIGN
909 SANSOME STREET
SAN FRANCISCO, CA 94111

GRAPHIC DESIGN
909 SANSOME STREET
SAN FRANCISCO, CA 94111
(415) 421-6321

HE'S ALL
WRITE!

MiKe

MIKE CONDON,INC.
CREATIVE COMMUNICATION SERVICES
1910 INGERSOLL AVE.
DES MOINES, IOWA 50309
515-244-1604

MIKE CONDON,INC.
CREATIVE COMMUNICATION SERVICES
1910 INGERSOLL AVE.
DES MOINES, IOWA 50309
515-244-1604

福德　佛　社

九龍呈翔道九號地段

Falcon Electronic Technologies, Inc.
1335 Winding Ridge
Colorado Springs, CO 80919

Falcon Electronic Technologies, Inc.
1335 Winding Ridge
Colorado Springs, CO 80919
Phone: 303-593-1470/0651
Tlx: 45 2440

RADIO SOLE 104.6

RADIO SOLE 104.6

RADIO SOLE s.r.l. Sede Legale: C.so d'Augusto, 26 47037 Rimini Tel. 0541/603081

Casella Postale 24 Rimini

RADIO SOLE s.r.l. Sede Legale: C.so d'Augusto, 26 47037 Rimini Tel. 0541/603081
Cap. Soc. L. 20.000.000 int. ver. Trib. di Rimini 5140 CCIAA Forlì 196385 Part. IVA 01004140404
Casella Postale 24 Rimini

«Albin Upp»
Galleri & Kunstkafé
Briskebyveien 42
Oslo 2

K. Bonnevie as
Telefon: 02/56 44 48
Bankgiro:
8540.08.01482

The Mickey Mantle Whitey Ford Fantasy Baseball Camp

P.O. Box 2500
Ashland, KY 41105-2500
(212) 382-1660

You'll receive instruction from and play against
your New York Yankee Heroes.

100 St. Andrews Boulevard, Naples, Florida 33942 • (813) 775-7661

AYESHA SONI
Photographer

'SAINARA', FLAT 101, CUFFE PARADE, COLABA, B'BAY 400 005. PHONE: 213536.

 Hemapheresis

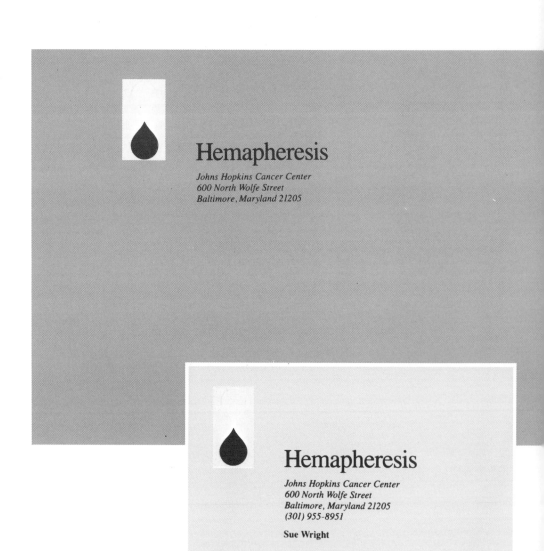

Hemapheresis

Johns Hopkins Cancer Center
600 North Wolfe Street
Baltimore, Maryland 21205

Hemapheresis

Johns Hopkins Cancer Center
600 North Wolfe Street
Baltimore, Maryland 21205
(301) 955-8951

Sue Wright

diane moon

graphics

714/646-7131
504 n. newport blvd.
ste. 202, newport beach
california 92663

24 Carrot
Gwenn Knight
Luckett Davidson
502: 637-7774

Le Café Musée
J. B. Speed Art Museum
2035 South Third Street
Louisville, Kentucky 40208
Reservations: 502: 637-7774
Catering: 502: 637-7774

Downstairs at Actors
Actors Theatre of Louisville
316 West Main Street
Louisville, Kentucky 40202
Reservations: 502: 584-1205
Bar: 502: 582-2364

Provident • Life Department • 1987 Convention

The Catalogue Group Inc.
142 FIFTH AVENUE NEW YORK, NEW YORK 10011
212 243 1200

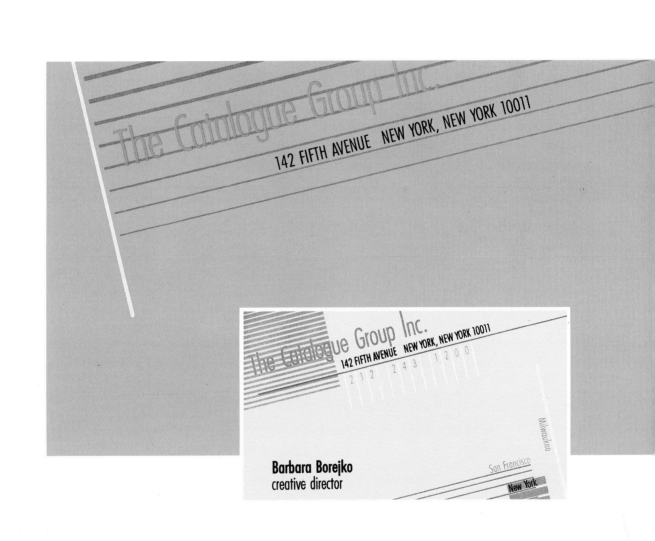

The Catalogue Group Inc.
142 FIFTH AVENUE   NEW YORK, NEW YORK 10011

The Catalogue Group Inc.
142 FIFTH AVENUE   NEW YORK, NEW YORK 10011
212 243 1200

Barbara Borejko
creative director

Milwaukee

San Francisco

New York

Milwaukee

San Francisco

New York

IRENE BORGER

451 21ST STREET
SANTA MONICA CA 90402
213.394.4201

IRENE BORGER · 451 21ST STREET · SANTA MONICA CA 90402

IRENE BORGER · 451 21ST STREET · SANTA MONICA CA 90402 · 213.394.4201

RAINBOW REAL ESTATE

1402 Montauk Highway, Mastic, New York 11950 (516) 281-3366

RAINBOW
REAL ESTATE

1402 Montauk Highway, Mastic, NY 11950

Sales — Rentals
Management

(516) 281-3366

RAINBOW
REAL ESTATE

Licensed Real Estate Broker

1402 Montauk Highway, Mastic, New York 11950

COOMBS

COOMBS
CONSULTING
LIMITED
P.O. BOX 4353
VANCOUVER
BRITISH COLUMBIA
CANADA
V6B 3Z7

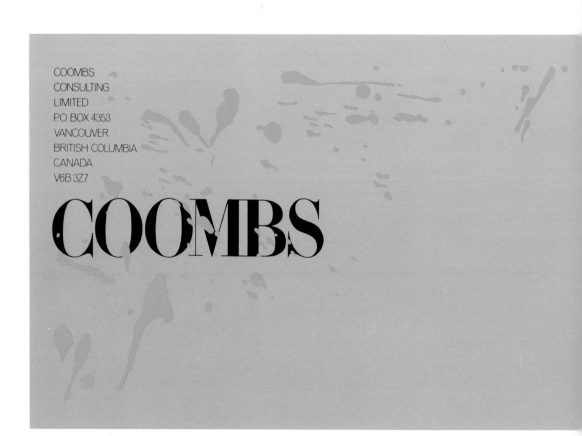

COOMBS
CONSULTING
LIMITED
P.O. BOX 4353
VANCOUVER
BRITISH COLUMBIA
CANADA
V6B 3Z7

COOMBS

J. DAVID SHAW
PRESIDENT

EARTH CONVERSIONS, INC.
"Purveyors of the Ultimate in Swimming Pools"
14505 TORREY CHASE BLVD. #108
(713) 583-1117   HOUSTON, TEXAS 77014

EARTH CONVERSIONS, INC.
"Purveyors of the Ultimate in Swimming Pools"
14505 TORREY CHASE BLVD. #108
HOUSTON, TEXAS 77014

EARTH
CONVERSIONS, INC.
*"Purveyors of the
Ultimate in Swimming Pools"*

J. DAVID SHAW
PRESIDENT

14505 TORREY CHASE BLVD. #108
HOUSTON, TEXAS 77014
(713) 583-1117

Jan Rieckhoff
Kielortallee 8
2000 Hamburg 13
☎ 040 45 20 38

OWENS
LUTTER

OWENS
LUTTER

3080 OLCOTT ST.
SUITE 200C
SANTA CLARA
CALIFORNIA 95051

3080 OLCOTT ST.
SUITE 200C
SANTA CLARA
CALIFORNIA 95051
(408) 496-0343

Paul Davis Studio   14 East 4th Street, New York, NY 10012, (212) 420·8789

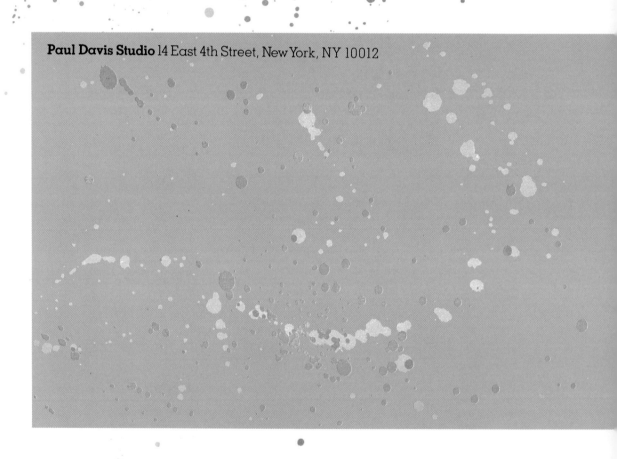

Paul Davis Studio 14 East 4th Street, New York, NY 10012

KAVITA SAHNI 161-D Dalamal Park Cuffe Parade Bombay-400 005 Phone: 212215

Triloka

Triloka Trading Co., Inc.

2901 Kuntz Avenue

Baltimore

Maryland 21207

U.S.A.

(301) 922-8225

Triloka

Triloka Trading Co., Inc.

2901 Kuntz Avenue

Baltimore

Maryland 21207

U.S.A.

LASER

JIM LASER
PHOTOGRAPHER

LASER

JIM LASER
PHOTOGRAPHER

THE LASER WORKS
ATELIER PHOTOGRAPHIQUE

WILDWOOD BEACH·HANSVILLE·WASHINGTON 98340
206 638 - 2131

THE LASER WORKS
ATELIER PHOTOGRAPHIQUE

WILDWOOD BEACH·HANSVILLE·WASHINGTON 98340
206 638 - 2131

OHIO PRINTING COMPANY LTD.

Rudy Schmidt
President

145 North Grant Avenue
Columbus, Ohio 43215
614/224-1257

OHIO PRINTING COMPANY LTD. • 145 North Grant Avenue • Columbus, Ohio 43215

OHIO PRINTING COMPANY LTD. • 145 North Grant Avenue • Columbus, Ohio 43215 • 614/224-1257

QUOTATION

Estimate Number

To

We are pleased to submit our estimate for the following:

Description

Quantity

Stock

Number of Colors

Size
Flat
Folded

Number of Pages

Bindery

Price

Miscellaneous

Terms Net 30 days F.O.B. Columbus, Ohio   30 day limitation on price listed above

The above prices have been estimated from: ☐ Rough Sketch   ☐ Comprehensive Layout   ☐ Final Art

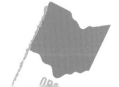

COPY A

Freddie Reding
Writer/Producer
3103 Eisenhauer Rd. #J4
San Antonio, Texas 78209
512/824-9355

COPY A

Freddie Reding
Writer/Producer
3103 Eisenhauer Rd. #J4
San Antonio, Texas 78209
512/824-9355

CLAUSEN ADVERTISING

341 NORTH MAPLE DR., SUITE 410A, BEVERLY HILLS, CA. 90210

CLAUSEN ADVERTISING

341 NORTH MAPLE DR., SUITE 410A, BEVERLY HILLS, CA. 90210

213/550-0496

TELEX 194449 or 4720127 ATTN:DC

P.O. BOX 561925
MIAMI, FLA. 33156
(305) 665-1900

HOLLYWOOD, KENTUCKY

Post Office Box 2500 □ Ashland, Kentucky 41105-2500 □ Telephone: (606) 329-0077

A Television Production Company

HOLLYWOOD KENTUCKY

A Television Production Company

Genesis Entertainment
A Division of
Gannaway Enterprises, Incorporated
5743 Corsa Ave. • Suite 210
Westlake Village, CA 91362

Genesis Entertainment
A Division of Gannaway Enterprises, Incorporated

5743 Corsa Ave. • Suite 210 Westlake Village, CA 91362 • Telephone: 818-706-6341

Miami Children's Hospital
6125 Southwest 31st Street
Miami, Florida 33155, USA

John Leffler

MUSIC, INC.

161 W. 22 ST. N.Y.C. 10011 212.546.1515 255.3043

ITAOCAMBA

DISCOS & PRODUÇÕES ARTÍSTICAS LTDA.

Paul Pullara
Graphic Design
10 Walnut Street
Little Falls, NJ 07424
201 785 3250

Paul Pullara
Graphic Design
10 Walnut Street
Little Falls, NJ 07424

COLORBAND:USA

COLORBAND:USA

7729 Lockheed
Suite C
El Paso, Texas 79925
915 - 778-1337

7729 Lockheed
Suite C
El Paso, Texas 79925
915 - 778-1337

KRISTI JOHNSON SIMKINS DESIGN

269 Columbus Avenue
Tuckahoe, NY 10707
914-793-0583

KRISTI JOHNSON SIMKINS DESIGN

269 Columbus Avenue
Tuckahoe, NY 10707
914-793-0583

KRISTI JOHNSON SIMKINS DESIGN

269 Columbus Avenue
Tuckahoe, NY 10707
914-793-0583

KRISTI JOHNSON SIMKINS DESIGN

269 Columbus Avenue
Tuckahoe, NY 10707
914-793-0583

KRISTI JOHNSON SIMKINS DESIGN

269 Columbus Avenue
Tuckahoe, NY 10707
914-793-0583

KRISTI JOHNSON SIMKINS DESIGN

269 Columbus Avenue
Tuckahoe, NY 10707
914-793-0583

KRISTI JOHNSON SIMKINS DESIGN

269 Columbus Avenue
Tuckahoe, NY 10707
914-793-0583

KRISTI JOHNSON SIMKINS DESIGN

269 Columbus Avenue
Tuckahoe, NY 10707
914-793-0583

KRISTI JOHNSON SIMKINS DESIGN

269 Columbus Avenue
Tuckahoe, NY 10707
914-793-0583

KRISTI JOHNSON SIMKINS DESIGN

269 Columbus Avenue
Tuckahoe, NY 10707
914-793-0583

KRISTI JOHNSON SIMKINS DESIGN

N. 6517 Greenwood Blvd.
Spokane, Washington
99205

(509) 326-2224

THE HOSPITAL
FOR SICK CHILDREN
CENTRE.

555 University Avenue
Toronto, Ontario M5G 1X8
(416) 598-6222
Charitable Registration No. 0003160-10-13

HELP US BUILD IT FOR THE CHILDREN.

THE FRAMEMAKER

THE FINEST IN CREATIVE FRAMING

THE FRAMEMAKER

THE FINEST IN CREATIVE FRAMING

Century Plaza, Suite 605
Wichita Falls, Texas 76308

LAWRENCE ROSS
PUBLISHING

9601 Wilshire Boulevard
Beverly Hills, California 90210
213/274-5590

Larry A. Ross
President

LAWRENCE ROSS
PUBLISHING

9601 Wilshire Boulevard
Beverly Hills, California 90210
213/274-5590

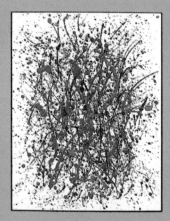

LAWRENCE ROSS
PUBLISHING

9601 Wilshire Boulevard
Beverly Hills, California 90210

PEARCE

S U R V E Y O R S

V A L U E R S

COMMERCIAL & RESIDENTIAL
E S T A T E   A G E N T S

Pearce & Co. 64 Guildford Street, Chertsey, Surrey KT16 9BD. Telephone Chertsey (09328) 61221
Partners: JR Hedges FSVA ARVA D J Wareham Dip.Est.Man.ARICS **Consultants:** R Pearce FRICS R G Stevenson FSVA
Ross P Ballerino ARICS

——— Year 22 ———
STATE OF THE ART

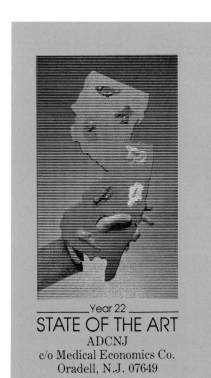

——— Year 22 ———
STATE OF THE ART
ADCNJ
c/o Medical Economics Co.
Oradell, N.J. 07649

Art Directors Club of New Jersey
c/o Medical Economics Company
Oradell, New Jersey 07649
201-262-3030

BURDETT
OPTICAL COMPANY LTD
SPECTACLE FRAME DESIGNERS & MANUFACTURERS

24 Mowlem Street London E2 9HE Telephone 01-980 2638 Telex 919031
Registered No. 399970 London

Shot in the Dark Studios
1255 University Avenue
Rochester, New York 14607
716-244-6334

Shot in the Dark Studios
1255 University Avenue
Rochester, New York 14607

Mail Station 440
200 Smith Street
Waltham, MA 02154

The Breakers, April 24-28, 1983

3384 Peachtree Road, N.E.
Suite 717
Atlanta, Georgia 30326

富洋水族工程有限公司
Artocean Aquarium Engineering Ltd.
186-188 Lockhart Road, Wanchai, Hong Kong
Tel: 5-732692 Telex: 54427 ONTCO HX

A Professional
Corporation

595
North Westwind Dr.
El Cajon, California
92020

A Professional
Corporation

595
North Westwind Dr.
El Cajon, California
92020

619 442-0983

Lemons
Communications
Group inc.

3501 N. MacArthur Blvd.
Suite 417
Irving, Texas 75062
214/252-7519

Lemons
Communications
Group inc.

3501 N. MacArthur Blvd.
Suite 417
Irving, Texas 75062
214/252-7519

Stacy Lemons
Executive Vice-President

Lemons
Communications
Group inc.

3501 N. MacArthur Blvd.
Suite 417
Irving, Texas 75062

VISION

Vision Gallery, Inc.
1151 Mission Street
San Francisco, CA 94103

VISION

Edward Donhowe,
Manager

Vision Gallery, Inc.
1151 Mission Street
San Francisco, CA 94103
(415) 621-2107

Vision Gallery, Inc.
1151 Mission Street
San Francisco, CA 94103
(415) 621-2107

Frances Lee Jasper
Oriental Rugs

Frances Lee Jasper
Oriental Rugs

Quad 7
1330 Bardstown Road
Louisville
Kentucky 40204
502 459-1044

Carl J. Johns
Manager
Operational Services

HoTelNet
1809 DeLeon Street
Tampa, Florida 33606
813/254-1797

SwanValley
At Breckenridge

SwanValley
At Breckenridge

Breckenridge Associates, Inc.
Box 8175 Breckenridge, CO 80424
303 453-4000, 800 525-2253

THE
DESIGN OFFICE
OF
JOSEPH FEIGENBAUM

30 EAST
37TH STREET
NEW YORK
NEW YORK
10016
212·685·1178

THE
DESIGN OFFICE
OF
JOSEPH FEIGENBAUM

30 EAST
37TH STREET
NEW YORK
NEW YORK
10016

THE
DESIGN OFFICE
OF
JOSEPH FEIGENBAUM
30 EAST
37TH STREET
NEW YORK,
NEW YORK
10016
212·685·1178

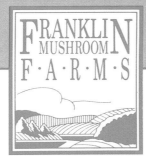

P.O. Box 18
North Franklin,
Connecticut 06254
203-642-7551

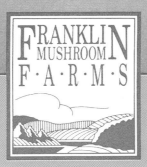

P.O. Box 18
North Franklin,
Connecticut 06254

Graphic Design

Elaine Pantages
7002 Boulevard East
Guttenberg, N.J. 07093
(201) 861-7609

Graphic Design

Elaine Pantages. 7002 Boulevard East. Guttenberg. N.J. 07093

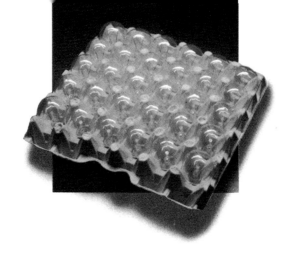

特高廣告有限公司・香港灣仔謝斐道一五一號金聲大廈三樓Ａ座

the group advertising limited · 2a kam sing mansion, 151 jaffe road, wanchai, hong kong · phone: 5-8912013

2029 CENTURY PARK EAST
SUITE 1110
LOS ANGELES, CALIFORNIA 90067

Mr. Thomas D. O'Connor
President
Mohawk Paper Mills
Cohoes, New York 12047

Dear Mr. O'Connor:

In our business, we live to sing the praises of a masterpiece.
To admire the genius it represents. And to feel the emotion it
expresses.

Recently we had the opportunity to do just that. But the work was
not a creation of Rembrandt, Monet or Renoir. It was your new
Mohawk Nuance Cover, Text, and Writing paper. We knew immediately
that this is the paper upon which all future communications of the
Metro Museum of Modern Art will be printed.

We were delighted to learn that at last there is a paper that lives
up to all of our standards. Nuance has a distinguished yet
personable look, thanks to its light linen mark which strikes a
perfect balance between subtlety in color and depth of finish. We
were pleased to find that it's acid, alum and rosin free, and that
it embodies the qualities of longevity, optimum printabilty and
value we've come to expect and appreciate in Mohawk papers.

What's more, Nuance is versatile. We're using Alpine White 70 lb.
Text for our letterhead, and we'll be selecting from your wide range
of other weights for our envelopes, calling cards, brochures, and
annual report. And those colors--magnifique! (We even adopted them
for our palette imprint below!)

I think you can sense our enthusiasm for Nuance. Here at the museum
we pride ourselves in displaying the best names in our business.
You obviously take pride in being the best name in yours.

Sincerely,

Claude Artemus Nouveau
Director of Museum Imagery

Hello, good buy.

A lot of people think Hammermill Bond beats other bond sheets coming and going.

You see, Hammermill Bond comes with a watermark known and respected in business for the best part of a century. As well as the rich look and crisp feel your clients expect from the most expensive writing and printing papers.

Yet it goes for considerably less than they expect to pay. And that's why they'll consider it such a good, good buy.

Hammermill Bond gives your clients a combination of quality, economy and more colors, weights and finishes to choose from than practically any bond sheet on the market. So it's ideal for letterheads. And for matching envelopes, bulletins, releases and wherever else first impressions count.

Next project, recommend the world's best-known business paper: Hammermill Bond. And you could find yourself saying hello to some extra assignments.

Let Hammermill do the paper work.

Graham Catlin+Associates

Your ref

Our ref

Date

Rathlin House
Elm Road
Horsell, Woking
Surrey GU21 4DY
England

Telephone:
Woking 23735/6
Area code (04862)

Telex: 859135 Catlin G
Cable:'Greycat Woking'

Partners
G Catlin
L J A Catlin

Registered address
As above

Registered number
2454852 (England)

Wilson & Wilson ▪ Advertising and Public Relations

Wilson & Wilson ▪ Advertising and Public Relations

507 Granger Terrace, Suite 4 ▪ Sunnyvale, California 94087

CHAFFEY CORPORATION
BASEBALL CLUB

17249 NE 116th STREET, REDMOND, WASHINGTON 98052. (206) 883-2412.

Hosts of the 1985 Senior Babe Ruth Pacific Northwest Regional Tournament.
Senior Babe Ruth World Series Participants 1981, 1982, 1984.

FOR KIDS ONLY
PRODUCTIONS

FKO

FOR KIDS ONLY PRODUCTIONS

1318 W. TOUHY, #C • CHICAGO, IL 60626

PRAIRIE LANDS CLASSIC

PRO-AM GOLF TOURNAMENT

Post Office Box 1541
Champaign, Illinois 61820
217 359-1088

COMMITTEE MEMBERS

Michael R. Byrd
Chairman
B.S. Productions

Bart Collins
International
Management Group

Sue Dawson
Mercy Hospital

Tom Ealy
Cozad Investment
Services

W. Frank Elston
Servants United
Foundation

Robert Metcalf
Urbana Golf &
Country Club

Colleen Murphy
Mercy Hospital

Tim Murphy
Eisner Murphy Piper

Penn Nelson
Norrell Temporary
Employment Services

Steve Shanks
R & M Golf Supply

Brad Sussman
WKIO Radio

Actus Dance Institute   49 Summerhill Avenue, Toronto, Ontario M4T 1A9   Telephone (416) 929-0405

ACTUS

Actus Dance Institute
49 Summerhill Avenue, Toronto, Ontario M4T 1A9
Telephone (416) 929-0405

DATAMATION SERVICES, INC.

DATALINE SYSTEMS, INC.

7625 Rosecrans Avenue
Paramount, California 90723
(213) 634-3000

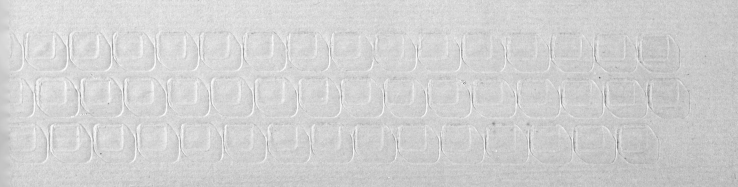

DATAMATION SERVICES, INC.

DATALINE SYSTEMS, INC.

7625 Rosecrans Avenue
Paramount, California 90723
(213) 634-3000

Telecommunications Consultive Services 555 N. New Ballas, Suite 310, Saint Louis, MO 63141   314-569-8578

THE
SEIDEMAN
COMPANY

THE
SEIDEMAN
COMPANY
*Telecommunications
Consultive Services*

PATRICIA C. SEIDEMAN

*555 N. New Ballas, Suite 310
Saint Louis, MO 63141
314-569-8578*

THE
SEIDEMAN
COMPANY

*555 N. New Ballas, Suite 310
Saint Louis, MO 63141*

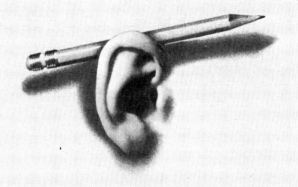

Allan Niilo illustration and design 2-2635 Granville St., Vancouver, B.C. V6H 3H2 733-1261

Summer at the Centre
L'été chaud du Centre

National
Arts
Centre

Centre
national
des Arts

Box 1534
Station B
Ottawa, Ontario
K1P 5W1
(613) 996-5051

CP 1534
succursale B
Ottawa, Ontario
K1P 5W1
(613) 996-5051

DESIGN IN ACTION

14-16 PETERBOROUGH ROAD LONDON SW6 3BN
TELEPHONE 01 731 0254 TELEX 8811684 TELECOPIER 017333

DIRECTORS P. THOMAS (CHAIRMAN) B. SALTER (MANAGING) G. DENHAM J. CASTLE
DESIGN IN ACTION LIMITED REGISTERED OFFICE 63 St MARTIN'S LANE LONDON WC2N 4JS COMPANY REGISTRATION NUMBER 1615858 (ENGLAND)

Advertising/Marketing for

Motion Pictures, Television

& Cable Systems

2205 North Dymond Street

Burbank, California

91505

213 / 846-0698

Quixote.

SOUTHERN
HEALTH
SERVICES

8600 Quioccasin Road
Suite 201-A
Richmond, Virginia 23229
804/740-4206

Board of Directors

Herbert A. Claiborne, Jr., M.D.
John M. Daniel, III, M.D.
Ronald K. Davis, M.D.
Emerson D. Farley, Jr., M.D.
Darrell K. Gilliam, M.D.
Samuel M. Janney, II, M.D.
Manikoth G. Kurup, M.D.
C. M. Kinloch Nelson, M.D.
Charles H. Robertson, Jr., M.D.
Giles M. Robertson, Jr., M.D.
Edward M. Saylor, M.D.
Lindley T. Smith, M.D.
Marvin L. Weger, M.D.
Richard L. Worland, M.D.

Howard J. Newman
President

8600 Quioccasin Road
Suite 201-A
Richmond, Virginia 23229

SOUTHERN
HEALTH
SERVICES

Southern Health
Management Corporation:
General Partner

PETER KERR DESIGN ASSOCIATES LTD

GRAPHIC DESIGN · PACKAGE DESIGN · PRODUCT DESIGN · INTERIOR DESIGN

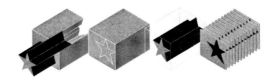

89a Quicks Road, Wimbledon, London SW19 1EX, England. Telephone 01-540 9884

Spanish Office: Tellagorri – El Golf, Apartado 24, Fuenterrabia, Spain. Telephone 010 34 43 61 80 99 Telex 36143 Bader E
Directors: P B Kerr MSIAD, J M Kerr **Associate directors:** G Capdevila MSIAD Mdes RCA, G J Lyle, W S L Ingleton BA
Registered address: 50a Downing Street, Farnham, Surrey GU9 7PH. Registered number: 1343327 (England)

ULTRON

Ultron Technologies
Corporation

One World Trade Center
Suite 7967
New York, NY 10048

Tel: (212) 775-1200
    (212) 524-7722

Telex: 126394

ULTRON

Ultron Technologies
Corporation

One World Trade Center
Suite 7967
New York, NY 10048

ABRAHAM GLASS
Managing Director

ULTRON

Ultron Technologies
Corporation

One World Trade Center
Suite 7967
New York, NY 10048

Tel: (212) 775-1200
    (212) 524-7722
Telex: 126394

INTERNATIONAL BANK
OF THE SOUTH PACIFIC

INTERNATIONAL BANK
OF THE SOUTH PACIFIC

FAKAFANUA CENTER
P.O. BOX 1401
NUKU'ALOFA
TONGA

FAKAFANUA CENTRE
P.O. BOX 1401
NUKU'ALOFA,
TONGA
TELE: 22-200

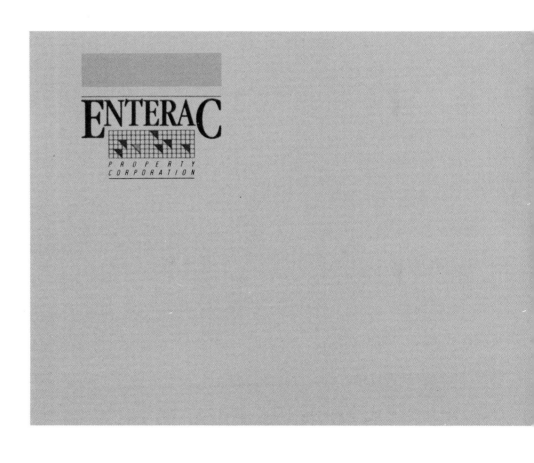

Greg Newman

1356 Brampton Road   Pasadena   California 91105   (213) 257-6247

Greg
Newman

Greg
Newman

PRIVATE SHOWING

fine european lingerie

Wayne
Pederson
Graphic
Design &
Consultation

1531 Packard
Ann Arbor
Michigan 48104
313 995 0240
668 0559
212 825 5507

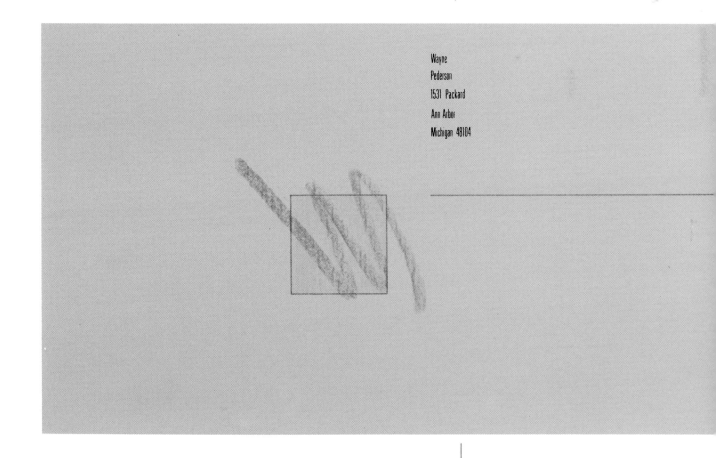

Wayne
Pederson
1531 Packard
Ann Arbor
Michigan 48104

Wayne
Pederson
Graphic
Design &
Consultation

**Eagle Pacific
Insurance Company**

2000
Fourth & Blanchard Bldg.
Seattle, WA 98121

2000
Fourth & Blanchard Bldg.
Seattle, WA 98121
(206) 682-6636

RIVERPARC

RIVERPARC

Ballet
Coppélia

Rua Carme Maito Stinglin,75
Portão/Fone: 242-9905/Curitiba
Cep:80.000
Insc.Sec.Educação 1330
CGC 76.754.407/0001-76

J June Haywood

U 1095 Pensive Lane

N Great Falls, Virginia

E 22066

703 759 6978

22 EAST 13TH STREET   NEW YORK 10003

NATIONAL
CHILD WATCH
CAMPAIGN

National Center for Missing and Exploited Children
National Child Safety Council
American Gas Association

NATIONAL
CHILD WATCH
CAMPAIGN

National Office—P.O. Box 1368, Jackson, Michigan 49204

National Office—P.O. Box 1368, Jackson, Michigan 49204   Tel. (800) 222-1464

THE SPORTS CLUB/LA

THE SPORTS CLUB/LA

1835 Sepulveda Blvd.
West Los Angeles, CA. 90025
(213) 473-1447

Editor/Writer

Tish Young McCutchen

1924 Clairmont Road, Suite 110
Decatur, Georgia 30033
404-633-3089

Editor/Writer

Tish Young McCutchen

1924 Clairmont Road, Suite 110
Decatur, Georgia 30033
404-633-3089

Matthew Klein Studio *15 West 18th Street, 10th Floor, New York, New York 10011 Telephone (212) 255-6400* **Photography**

Matthew Klein Studio

Matthew Klein Studio   15 West 18th Street, 10th Floor, New York, New York 10011   **Photography**

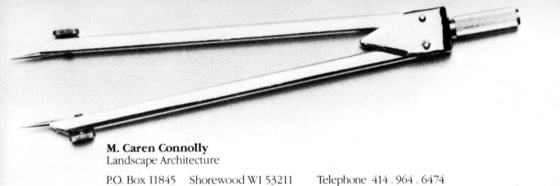

M. Caren Connolly
Landscape Architecture

P.O. Box 11845   Shorewood WI 53211   Telephone 414 . 964 . 6474

P.O. Box 11845   Shorewood WI 53211

M. Caren Connolly
Landscape Architecture

P.O. Box 11845   Shorewood WI 53211   Telephone 414 . 964 . 6474

M. Caren Connolly

Mercedez Leoms Game<u>S</u>iro
redatora Revizora

R

Rua Princesa Isabel, 415 - Curitiba - PR.

Psychiatric Diagnostic Laboratories of America, Inc. • 47 Maple Street • Summit, New Jersey 07901 • 201-522-7043

Miran
(Oswaldo Miranda)

Estúdio de Arte
Art Studio
Curitiba (Brasil)
New York (USA)

JOHN P. KNUTSON

Business:
Route 7, Pine Point Road
Menomonie, Wisconsin 54751
Telephone: 715-235-6169

Residence:
Telephone: 715-235-6040

Graphics One

Carlos Grasseti

Diretor de Arte
Revista Playboy (São Paulo)

RICHARD HATCH

501 Woodland
Houston, Texas 77009

501 Woodland
Houston, Texas 77009
(713) 862~6108

PETER RAVN DESIGN

STRANDGADE 10B · 1401 KØBENHAVN K · 01·57 31 31

Atelier
Rua Senador Vergueiro, 137
Apt. 101

PotyLazzarotto. *Rua Senador Vergueiro, 66*
Apt. 702
Fone: 225-2435
Rio de Janeiro.

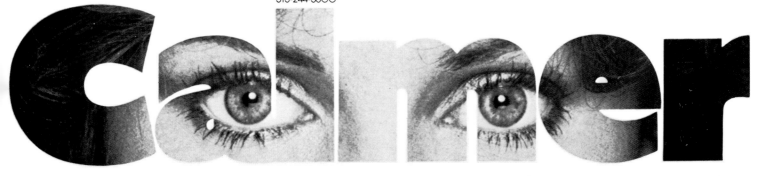

BOB CALMER PHOTOGRAPHY
No. 1 11TH STREET
11TH & CHERRY
DES MOINES, IOWA 50309
515-244-5500

The QUORUM

17th Floor, United Bank Tower, 15th & Guadalupe
Austin, Texas 78701   512/472-6779

Banquet Facilities & Catering

Gráfica

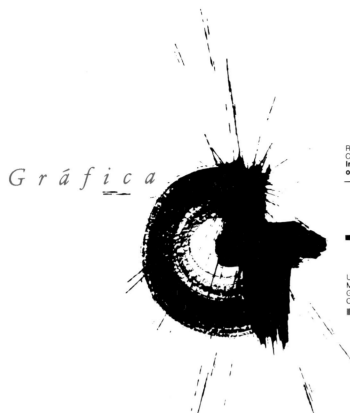

Revista Internacional de
Comunicação Visual.
**International Quarterly Magazine
of the Visual Communication**

GRÁFICA

Uma publicação de
Miran Estúdio, Editora&Art Shop Ltda.
Galeria Schaffer, Lj. 6
Curitiba/Pr/Brasil 80.000

Uwe Schmidt
Garten und
Landschaftsbau,
Baumpflege.

J6, 2
6800 Mannheim
Telefon
0621-15580

Dresdner Bank
(BLZ 670 800 50)
Konto:
7112 920

Penguin
RECORDING

Owner
John Strother
P.O. Box 91332 Pasadena, California   91109-1332   (213) 259-8612

WILFRIED WOLTER, FOTOGRAF

4000 Düsseldorf, Florastraße 12, Telefon (0211) 37 06 09
Commerzbank Düsseldorf: Nr. 56 58 950, BLZ 300 400 00

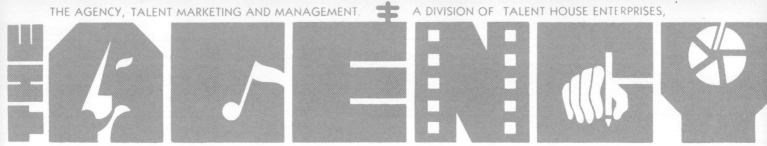

DINERS BUSINESS SERVICES PRIVATE LIMITED, 213 RAHEJA CHAMBERS, NARIMAN POINT, BOMBAY 400 021. TEL: 245383/245197.

THE AGENCY, TALENT MARKETING AND MANAGEMENT.   A DIVISION OF TALENT HOUSE ENTERPRISES,

7104 Langston Drive
Austin, Texas 78723
512 926-1765

Vitale&Associates
Communication Design

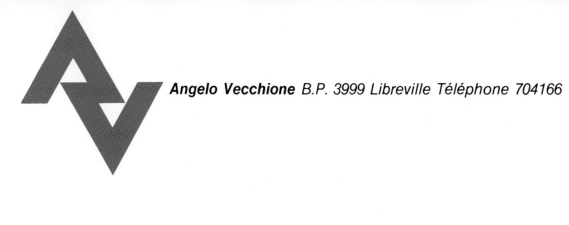

Angelo Vecchione B.P. 3999 Libreville Téléphone 704166

Festival International
de Commedia dell'Arte
du Val de Marne

Directeur:
Marcel Tavé
Direction Artistique ACDA:
Carlo Fortunato
Innocente Salvoni
Administrateur Général:
Ivan Maletti

Théâtre Romain Rolland
18 rue Eugène Varlin
94800 Villejuif
Tél. 7261502 / 7260812

NATIONAL SELF-HELP CENTER
FOR THE DEAF/HEARING-IMPAIRED

P.O. Box 33039 • Austin, Texas 78764 • 1-800-252-7034 • (512) 443-3323

4605 Post Oak Place
PO Box 27608
Houston, TX 77027

Eugene L. Butler
President and
Chief Operating Officer

713 621 8500

Weatherford

4605 Post Oak Place
PO Box 27608
Houston, TX 77027

Weatherford

robert Minuzzo

INDUSTRIAL CENTER BUILDING RM 350 SAUSALITO CA 94965 (415) 332 9916

PIPER TRUST

EYTAN KAUFMAN ·
DESIGN AND DEVELOPMENT
101 FIFTH AVENUE
NEW YORK NY 10003 ·
212/691 1607

ACARE

AMERICAN CARDIAC
REHABILITATION CENTERS, INC.

1106 Clayton Lane • Suite 410 E. • Austin, Texas 78723 • (512) 450-1188

COLUMBIA ALBUMS

GIRISH C. JOSHI DIRECTOR

106, BHANDARI STREET, BOMBAY 400 003, (INDIA). TELEX: 011 71931 KCCO IN ● 011 3713 KCCO IN ● CABLE: IMPROVED
DELHI ● PANIPAT (HARYANA) ● BARDOLI (GUJARAT) PHONE 326913 338565 5129834 5126237

**Commerce Park at
Middleborough Circle**

*Commerce Park Corporation
Member NAIOP*

*43 East Grove Street
Middleborough, MA 02346*

617-947-5565

**Commerce Park at
Middleborough Circle**

*Commerce Park Corporation
Member NAIOP*

43 East Grove Street

Mailing Address: *P.O. Box 1225, Middleborough, MA 02346.*

575 FIFTH AVENUE   NEW YORK, NEW YORK 10036   212-972-2020   TELEX:6720425BR/PLA   FAX:212-682-6917

ARTHURS,
BIEDRYCKI
&
ASSOCIATES

1009 East Blvd./Charlotte, NC 28203/(704) 333-0503

Main Office:
1333 F Street, N.W.
Washington, D.C. 20005
(202) 737-7900

U.S. & International
Trademark Searching

1333 F Street, N.W.
Washington, D.C. 20005

739 BRYANT STREET
SAN FRANCISCO 94107

415/495-6280

A service of Home Box Office, Inc.   1100 Avenue of the Americas   New York, NY 10036   212·512·1000   **Media Relations**

G R O U P T H I N K ™

A few good ideas about advertising, public relations and marketing communications.

The Adams Group, Inc.
100 Park Avenue
Rockville, Maryland 20850

The Adams Group, Inc., publishes GROUPTHINK for clients and other friends.

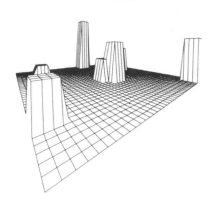

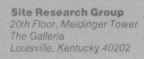

Site Research Group
20th Floor, Meidinger Tower
The Galleria
Louisville, Kentucky 40202

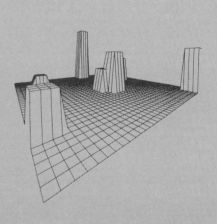

Site Research Group
20th Floor, Meidinger Tower
The Galleria
Louisville, Kentucky 40202
(502)581-0091

Robert K. Miller   880 Laurel Lane ♠ Northbrook, IL 60062 ♠ 312/272-3850

MIRACLES BY
APPOINTMENT

Lifespring Central Office
4340 Redwood Highway, Suite 50
San Rafael, California 94903
(415) 479-7873

L I F E S P R I N G

Central Office
4340 Redwood Highway, Suite 50
San Rafael, California 94903

L I F E S P R I N G

Architectural Book Center
Colony Square
Retail Mall/Mall Level
1197 Peachtree Street, N.E.
Atlanta, GA 30361
404/873-3207

ORION METALS, INC.
5077 KINGSTON STREET
DENVER, COLORADO 80239
(303) 373-0820

Jack Stone Graphic Design
1513 South Fourth Street
Philadelphia, Penna. 19147
215-755-0468

jack•stone (jak′stōn′)

**Cellular
One**

P.O. Box 9159
Seattle, WA 98109-0159

P.O. Box 9159
Seattle, WA 98109-0159
201 Elliott Avenue West, Suite 220
Seattle, WA 98119-4216
206-284-5555

NATIVE TREE

Natural Resource Managers

Native Tree, Inc.
3900 McGinnis Ferry Road
at Georgia 400
Alpharetta, Georgia 30201

404-475-2555

ADAM JAMES

59 Gilpin Avenue
PO Box 11248
Hauppauge NY 11788
516 582 4300

ADAM JAMES

59 Gilpin Avenue
PO Box 11248
Hauppauge NY 11788

CARMICHÆL'S

Carmichael's Bookstore
1295 Bardstown Road
Louisville
Kentucky
40204

Telephone
502 456-6950

BOOKSTORE

 **Mark Lewis *Design*** Graphic/Environmental Design 8330 Draper Lane
& Consultant Silver Spring, Maryland 20910
301.589.3292

—

 Mark Lewis *Design* Graphic/Environmental Design 8330 Draper Lane
& Consultant Silver Spring, Maryland 20910
301.589.3292

_____

_____

_____

_____

_____

Cash Lewman
Real Estate
1330 Cherokee Road
Louisville, Kentucky 40204
502: 456-4847

The BridgeWay

James T. Harper
Administrator

The BridgeWay BridgeWay Road Post Office Box 8500 Little Rock, Arkansas 72215

Airtel Plaza

A BEST WESTERN HOTEL

Airtel Plaza

A BEST WESTERN HOTEL

7277 Valjean Avenue, Van Nuys, CA 91406 (818) 905-1040

JOHN HORNALL
DESIGN WORKS

JOHN HORNALL
DESIGN WORKS

200 WEST MERCER, SUITE 102   SEATTLE, WASHINGTON 98119

200 WEST MERCER, SUITE 102   SEATTLE, WASHINGTON 98119   (206) 283-1856

JACK DAVIS GRAPHICS

JACK DAVIS GRAPHICS

1826 MAYNARD DRIVE R6   GRAPHIC DESIGN
CHAMPAIGN ILLINOIS 61821   ILLUSTRATION
                               CONSULTATION

Rick Sawyer, Inc.
P.O. Box 308
Spring, TX 77383

Saiki & Associates, Inc.
154 West 18th Street
New York, NY 10011
212/255-0466

Saiki & Associates, Inc.
154 West 18th Street
New York, NY 10011
212/255-0466

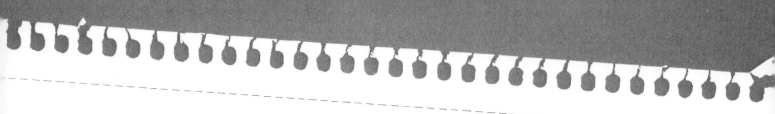

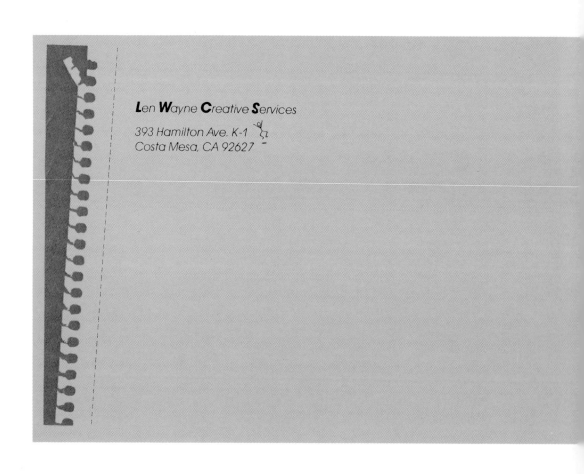

Len Wayne Creative Services

393 Hamilton Ave. K-1
Costa Mesa, CA 92627

n t

Nireu *José* **Teixeira**

n t

Nireu *José* **Teixeira**

Rua Desembargador
Vieira Cavalcanti, 760
Curitiba/Paraná
Cep: 80.000

GOLDMAZON
MINERAÇÃO DA AMAZÔNIA LTDA

GOLDMAZON
MINERAÇÃO DA AMAZÔNIA LTDA

Av. 7 de Setembro, 1321 – Centro
CEP 69000 – Manaus – Amazonas
Tels.: (092) 2322929 – 2320362
TELEX (092) 2504 MADM – BR

Av. 7 de Setembro, 1321 – Centro
CEP 69000 – Manaus – Amazonas
Tels.: (092) 2322929 – 2320362
TELEX (092) 2504 MADM – BR

ENTERTAINMENT MARKETING CONCEPTS · SUITE 804 · 2 WEST 46TH STREET · NEW YORK NY 10036 · 212·869·9733

Design/*International*

The Westin Building
P.O. Box 2028
Seattle, WA 98121

206.447.5000

International Telex
474 0126

Design/*International*

The Westin Building
P.O. Box 2028
Seattle, WA 98121

A Subsidiary of Westin Hotels

E.T. CRONIN
DESIGN

805 Avenue of the Americas
New York, New York 10001

SeaBank Savings, FSB
7400 North Kings Highway
Myrtle Beach, South Carolina 29577
(803) 449-9687

SEABANK®

SeaBank Savings, FSB
7400 North Kings Highway
Myrtle Beach, South Carolina 29577

N REF
DATA
OBJETO

Oz Comunicação Gráfica
Dr. Homem de Melo 875
Perdizes 05007
Fone (011) 62-7704
São Paulo SP

Oz Comunicação Gráfica
Dr. Homem de Melo 875
Perdizes 05007
Fone (011) 62-7704
São Paulo SP

Portland Museum
2308 Portland Avenue
Louisville, Kentucky 40212
(502) 776-7678

Brumunddal Frø

Frø, blomsterløk
planter og hageartikler
Grunnlagt 1895

Postboks 1
2381 Brumunddal, Norway
Telefon 065 / 41427
Bankgiro: 7192.05.00638
Postgiro: 5 40 70 28

Restaurant, Hotel,
Healthcare &
Uniform Services

224 Pontius North
Seattle, WA 98109
206.622.3600

NEW RICHMOND
SUPPLY LAUNDRIES

Restaurant, Hotel,
Healthcare &
Uniform Services

224 Pontius North
Seattle, WA 98109
206.622.3600

224 Pontius North
Seattle, WA 98109

NEW RICHMOND
SUPPLY LAUNDRIES

Ivy Healthcare Systems,
A Division Of Ivy International, Inc.

2010 Morton Drive
Post Office Box 5606
Charlottesville, Virginia 22905
(804) 979-2011

Ivy Healthcare Systems,
A Division Of Ivy International, Inc.

2010 Morton Drive
Post Office Box 5606
Charlottesville, Virginia 22905

Balans AS
Bygdøy allé 12, N - Oslo 2

Telefon 02/20 73 65
Telex 17564 Card n.
Bank 7032.05.51100.

Balans-
Alternativ sittestilling

The Widewaters Group

5794 Widewaters Parkway
Dewitt, NY 13214

The Widewaters Group
5794 Widewaters Parkway
Dewitt, N Y 13214
315/445-2424

Brian Marder, D.V.M.

Jonathan E. May, D.V.M.

Roslyn Veterinary Group

212 Mineola Avenue, Roslyn Heights, New York 11577 (516) 621-1744

The Woods Group, Inc.
1708 Whitehead Road
Baltimore, Maryland 21207
301 298 4700

The Woods Group, Inc.
1708 Whitehead Road
Baltimore, Maryland 21207

CLAYERS
Objects of Art

CLAYERS
Objects of Art

111-20 73rd Avenue Forest Hills, New York, 11375

111-20 73rd Avenue Forest Hills, New York, 11375 (212) 244-4270   Bob Costanza Gary Shillet

**Warkulwiz
Design
Associates**

*Graphic .
Communications*

123 S 22nd Street
Philadelphia, PA 19103

215-988-1777

**Warkulwiz
Design
Associates**

*Graphic
Communications*

123 S 22nd Street
Philadelphia, PA 19103

N A N C Y
S T E V E N S O N
1 0 9 W 2 8 S T
N E W Y O R K , N Y
1   0   0   0   1

N A N C Y
S T E V E N S O N
1 0 9 W 2 8 S T
N E W Y O R K , N Y
1   0   0   0   1
2 1 2 · 5 6 4 · 3 5 3 2

Myrna Davis
14 East 4th Street
New York, NY 10012
212 674·5708

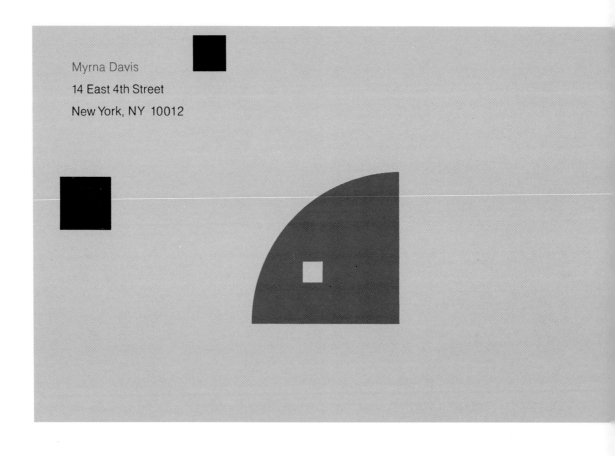

Myrna Davis
14 East 4th Street
New York, NY 10012

2912 WEST COMPTON BLVD
SUITE 204
GARDENA, CALIFORNIA 90249
TELEPHONE 538
2649

2912 WEST COMPTON BLVD
SUITE 204
GARDENA, CALIFORNIA 90249
TELEPHONE 538
2649

UMI DESIGN

UMI DESIGN

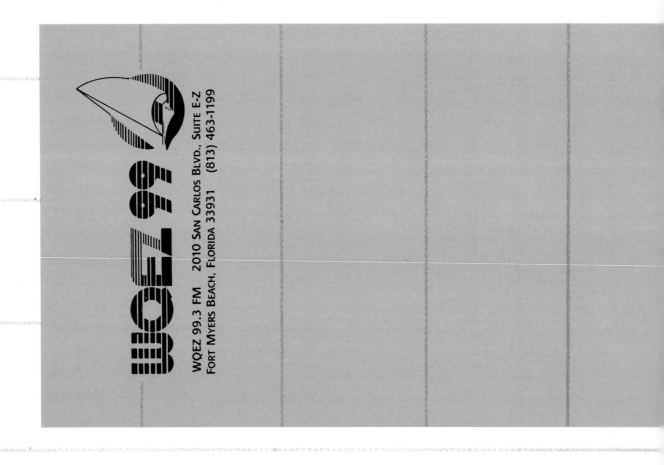

WQEZ 99.3 FM   2010 SAN CARLOS BLVD., SUITE E-Z
FORT MYERS BEACH, FLORIDA 33931   (813) 463-1199

Paris

Tony Paris Associates Inc.

137 East 25th Street
New York, New York 10010
Telephone: 212 686 6150

Multi-Media Communications

Paris

Tony Paris Associates Inc.   **137 East 25th Street**
New York, New York 10010

Rough Layout

PHOTO- GRAPHICS

RONNY SHINDER
46 Noble St. Studio 212
Toronto, Ontario M6K 2C9
(416) 535-0288

Rough Layout

PHOTO- GRAPHICS

RONNY SHINDER
46 Noble St. Studio 212
Toronto, Ontario M6K 2C9
(416) 535-0288

**Commercial
Lithographing
Company**

815 West Market Street   PO Box 1070
Louisville, KY 40201
502-583-1683

**Commercial
Lithographing
Company**

815 West Market Street   PO Box 1070
Louisville, KY 40201

Tania Energy, Inc.

Energy Exploration | 2122 Erin Way Glendale, California 91206

213•790-8600

Tania Energy, Inc.

2122
Erin Way
Glendale,
California 91206

Peter
Levenson

Peter
Levenson

Architect

300 East 34th Street
New York, NY 10016

Architect

300 East 34th Street
New York, NY 10016
212-889-8124

ZIRKLE LEE & ASSOCIATES, LTD.

4747 TABLE MESA DRIVE
SUITE 200
BOULDER, CO 80303
(303) 499-7790

ZIRKLE
LEE &
ASSOCIATES, LTD.

4747 TABLE MESA DRIVE
SUITE 200
BOULDER, CO 80303

Centre Dentaire Duquet

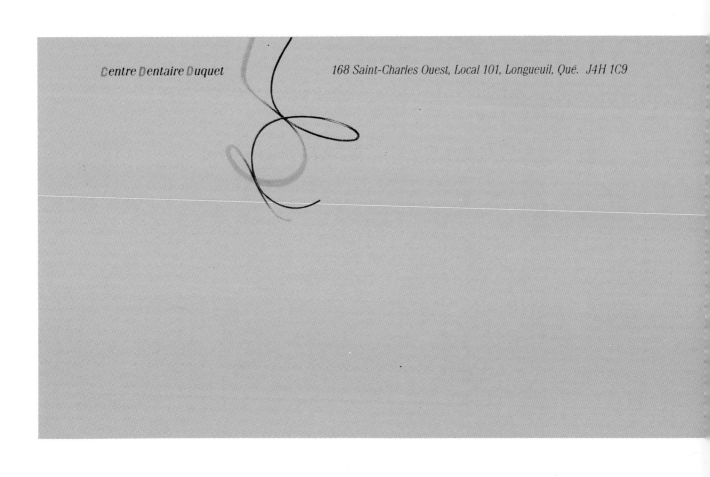

Centre Dentaire Duquet   *168 Saint-Charles Ouest, Local 101, Longueuil, Qué.   J4H 1C9*

168 Saint-Charles Ouest, Local 101, Longueuil, Qué.   J4H 1C9   (514) 463-1262

Glenridge Square
5395 Roswell Road, N.E.
Atlanta, GA 30342

789
456
123
ORCOLL •

**ORCOLL BUSINESS
SERVICE INC.**

ACCOUNTING
BOOKKEEPING
TAX WORK
FOR
SMALL BUSINESS

7750 ROUTE 30
N. HUNTINGDON,
PA 15642
412-863-1494

789
456
123
ORCOLL •

**ORCOLL BUSINESS
SERVICE INC.**

7750 ROUTE 30
N. HUNTINGDON,
PA 15642

The Eye

Suite 2005
100 Colony Square
Atlanta, Georgia 30361

404-881-8965

The Eye

Suite 2005
100 Colony Square
Atlanta, Georgia 30361

Graphic Ink
33 Commonwealth Road
Watertown, Ma 02172
617/923 9418

Graphic Ink
33 Commonwealth Road
Watertown, Ma 02172

NIKKI ALLYN GROSSO • SHERRE STOLLER

11630 CHAYOTE STREET • SUITE 2 • LOS ANGELES • CA • 90049 • MAILING ADDRESS • P.O. BOX 491246 • LOS ANGELES • CA • 90049 • TELEPHONE • 213 • 476 • 2893

MAILING ADDRESS • P.O. BOX 491246 • LOS ANGELES • CA • 90049

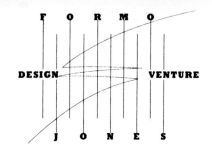

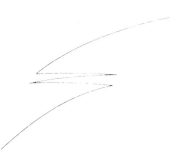

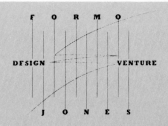

FORMO

DESIGN   VENTURE

JONES

460 WEST BROADWAY
NEW YORK, NEW YORK 10012

**Pedro Ho
Photography**

P.O. Box 597
Station Z
Toronto, Ontario,
Canada M5P 1P3
Tel: (416) 652-1425

**Pedro Ho
Photography**

P.O. Box 597
Station Z
Toronto, Ontario,
Canada M5P 1P3

Mike Hodges, Visual Communications   Post Office Box 390   University, MS 38677   601·234·5513

Mike Hodges, Visual Communications   Post Office Box 390   University, MS 38677   601·234·5513

ONE SERVICE

PLANEJAMENTO E CONTABILIDADE LTDA
Rua da Candelária 86 — 8.° andar
Tel.: 233-1691 e 233-3447

FORSYTHE·FRENCH·INC

Graphics for the Environment

4115 Broadway
Kansas City, Missouri 64111

816/561-6678

FORSYTHE·FRENCH·INC

4115 Broadway
Kansas City, Missouri 64111

Graphics for the Environment

4115 Broadway

Member of the Society of Environmental Graphics Designers

Ken Cato
Design Company
Pty Ltd

7.4 Bridport Street
Albert Park
Victoria 3206
Australia

Telephone
(03) 699 5488
Telex AA38209
CATHIB

GUTI PRODUÇÕES ARTÍSTICAS LTDA.

MCI
Communications
Corporation
1133 19th St. NW
Washington, DC 20036
202 887 2172

V. Orville Wright
President and
Chief Operating Officer

MCI
Communications
Corporation
1133 19th St. NW
Washington, DC 20036

MCI
Communications
Corporation
1133 19th St. NW
Washington, DC 20036

V. Orville Wright
President and
Chief Operating Officer

16812 A Red Hill Avenue ◆ Irvine, California 92714
(714) 261-1114 (714) 241-8668

Barbara P. Infranca

COMMONWEALTH INC.

3407 N. Kimball Avenue Chicago, Illinois 60618

Basys Inc.

2685 Marine Way
Mountain View
California
94043

415 969 9810

Telex 171604
BASYS MNTV

Basys Inc.

2685 Marine Way
Mountain View
California
94043

BASYS

2740 Miraloma · Anaheim, California 92806 **(714) 630-0910**

PRO·PACKAGING

José Luis Ortiz
Post Office Box 6678
Yorkville Finance Station
New York, NY 10128
212 831 6138

José Luis Ortiz
Post Office Box 6678
Yorkville Finance Station
New York, NY 10128

José Luis Ortiz
Post Office Box 6678
Yorkville Finance Station
New York, NY 10128
212 831 6138

LynnHaven
1600 Dodd Road
Winter Park, Florida
32792

Telephone
305-677-6842

PATRICIA RYAN SCHMIDT ▪▪ INTERIOR DESIGNER

PATRICIA RYAN SCHMIDT ▪ INTERIOR DESIGNER
6400 WEST MAIN ST., SUITE 1-J   BELLEVILLE, ILLINOIS 62223

6400 WEST MAIN ST., SUITE 1-J ▪▪ BELLEVILLE, ILLINOIS 62223   618-398-2727

Danica Meglič
izdelovanje preprostih drobnih kovinskih predmetov

jocova 43, 62000 maribor, tel. 062/31711

maribor, dne

Franc Ambrož – kleparstvo

Izdelava in montaža klimatskih in prezračevalnih naprav

Jurančičeva 7, 62000 Maribor, tel. 062/31-728
Bančni račun pri Jugobanki Maribor
51800-621-00063-8005-1430-05641/8

AMY FRIEDMAN·WRITER
198 COURT STREET #14
BROOKLYN NEW YORK 11201
718/625-2879

VonFeldt
GRAPHIC DESIGN

670 INCA
DENVER
COLORADO
80204
303 623 9024

SESAME SYSTEMS LTD. COMMERCIAL CENTER RAMAT-ILAN GIVAT SHMUEL 51905 ISRAEL TEL. 03 340962-6 TELEX: 341491

xavier-féal
designer

36, rue de picpus, 36
75012 paris 1.307 05 46

MIKE BERNE

COMMUNICATIONS

TRAVEL ASSOCIATES

1411 Fourth Avenue · Suite 620 · Seattle, Washington 98101 · (206) 623-5535

Claus F. Weidmüller, Polziner Straße 55 b, 2000 Hamburg 73

GLOBAL TRACING SERVICES INC.

P.O. BOX 69518
SEATTLE, WASHINGTON 98168
(206) 248-3130
TOLL FREE
1-800-663-6144

WORLD-WIDE SERVICE SINCE 1967

PORTAL

PORTAL PUBLICATIONS LTD., 21 TAMAL VISTA BOULEVARD, CORTE MADERA, CALIFORNIA 94925, 415-924-5652

Sereno Vianello
Vendita elettrodomestici
Assistenza tecnica

30010 Treporti (VE)
Via di Ca' Savio 32
Tel. (041) 658455

Cod. Fisc. VNL SRN 49M11 L736T
Part. IVA 00854740271

Data

casa

177 Stamford Street, Ashton-under-Lyne, Lancs OL6 7PS
Telephone 061-330 1067

CARROZZERIA JESOLANA s.d.f

30016 JESOLO (VE)
VIA MANTEGNA, 4
TEL. (0421) 951793
COD. FISC./PART. IVA 00712850270

DATA

POWDER MOUNTAIN RESORTS LTD

1360 - 200 Granville Street
Post Office Box 9
Vancouver, British Columbia
Canada V6C 1S4
Telephone: (604) 684-2515

University of Iowa *Hawkeyes*
Iowa City, Iowa 52240
Telephone 319 353 2121

Dept. of Athletics

University of Iowa *Hawkeyes*
Iowa City, Iowa 52240

Dept. of Athletics

WENDY GRIFFITH

29 S. 19th STREET · PHILADELPHIA, PA 19103

5 6 4 6 2 8 8

Child
Nutrition
Program

3921 Normal Street
San Diego, California
92103
(619) 294-2600

Child Nutrition Program
3921 Normal Street
San Diego, California 92103

Independent Pictures

Peter O'Brian Independent Pictures, Inc.
45 Charles St. East, Toronto, Canada M4Y 1S2
416-960-6468

**MARKET
DESIGN**

415/885·2610
1275 COLUMBUS AVENUE
SAN FRANCISCO, CA. 94133

MARKET DESIGN
1275 COLUMBUS AVENUE
SAN FRANCISCO, CA. 94133

415/885·2610
1275 COLUMBUS AVENUE
SAN FRANCISCO, CA. 94133

CAMPING
CA' PASQUALI

30010 TREPORTI (VENEZIA) - ITALIA
TEL. (041) 966110

DATA

SOCIETÁ TURISTICA DEL CAVALLINO

SEDE LEGALE: VENEZIA - SAN MARCO 3716/b - SEDE AMMINISTRATIVA: TREPORTI (VE) - VIA POERIO 33 - PARTITA IVA E CODICE FISCALE: 00170810279 - C.C.I.A.A. 65437

ANDREA SACHSE / 1565 NORTH CRANBROOK ROAD / BIRMINGHAM, MICHIGAN 48009 / (313) 645-2042

Agenzia Viaggi
DOGE GRITTI
30010 TREPORTI (VENEZIA) ITALIA
VIA FAUSTA 122 - TEL.(041)658312

DATA

Executive
Director
Stephen M.
Chandler

Reply Attention of:

The
chidren's
Aid Society of the County of Perth

380 Hibernia Street
Stratford, Ontario
N5A 5W3

Telephone:
(519) 271-5290

*Government Service
Insurance System*

Roman A. Cruz, Jr.
President

Roman A. Cruz, Jr.
President

*The
Government Service
Insurance System
Fourth Street
Metro Manila
Republic of the Philippines*

*The
Government Service
Insurance System
Fourth Street
Metro Manila
Republic of the Philippines
Telephone 47 17 30
Domestic Telex 2289/2290
International Telex 742 0139*

**FELLOWSHIP
BAPTIST
CHURCH**

"Loving the Lord – Loving Others"

REV. MICHAEL E. MAWHORTER
Pastor

77 Hornchurch Crescent
Markham, Ontario
L3R 4Z8
(416) 475-2007

Virginia Institute of
Marine Science

The
Virginia Institute of
Marine Science
Gloucester Point, Virginia 23062
Telephone 804 642 2111, 642 6131

The
Virginia Institute of
Marine Science
Gloucester Point, Virginia 23062

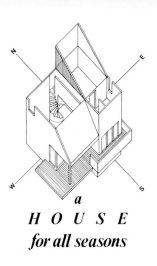

a
H O U S E
for all seasons

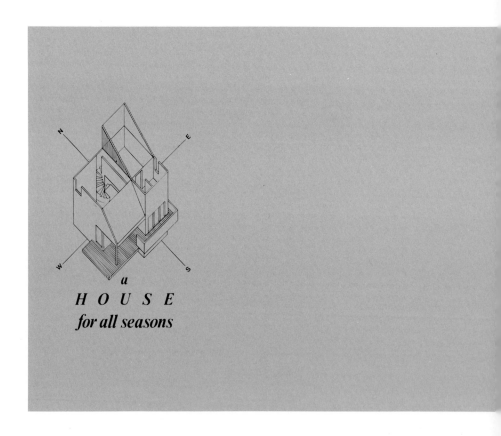

Channel Six, 1261 Glenarm Place, Denver, Colorado 80204 (303) 892-6666
"A House For All Seasons" is a production of KRMA-TV, Denver

Graphic Design Systems

270 Esna Park Drive #12
Markham, Ontario L3R 1H3
416 475-0300

Graphic Design Systems

270 Esna Park Drive #12
Markham, Ontario L3R 1H3
416 475-0300

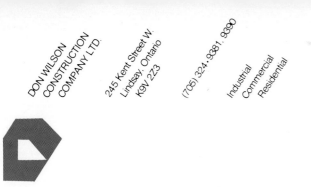

DON WILSON
CONSTRUCTION
COMPANY LTD.

245 Kent Street W.
Lindsay, Ontario
K9V 2Z3

(705) 324-9381 · 9390

Industrial
Commercial
Residential

Douglas Development Co.
2201 Martin
Irvine, California 92664
Telephone 714 833 2133

Robert W. White
President

Douglas Development Co.
2201 Martin
Irvine, California 92664

Robert W. White
President

Jeffery A. Yip
PHOTOGRAPHY

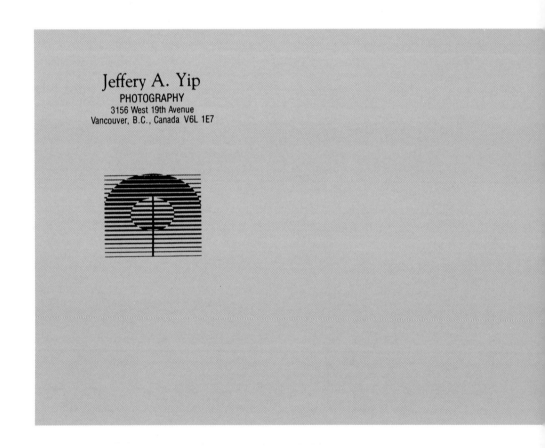

Jeffery A. Yip
PHOTOGRAPHY
3156 West 19th Avenue
Vancouver, B.C., Canada V6L 1E7

IMAGES /1-4-16·304 AZABUDAI MINATO-KU TOKYO JAPAN 〒106 PHONE:(03)583-9860

169 Cambria Street
Stratford, Ontario
N5A 1H6
519/273-1691

111 King Street East
Toronto, Ontario
M5C 1G6
416/363/2405

169 Cambria Street
Stratford, Ontario
N5A 1H6
519/273-1691

Lindemans legat
Norges musikkhøgskole
Nordahl Brunsgate 8, Oslo 1

Postadresse: «Jubileum 1983»
Postboks 6877, St. Olavs plass, N-Oslo 1
Telefon: 02/20 70 19

Fra konservatorium 1883
til høgskole 1973
100 år 1983

1883 Fra konservatorium
1973 til høgskole
1983 100 år

GLADE
Swimming Pools
LIMITED

1 Cutlers Croft Neptown Road
Henfield West Sussex
Telephone 0273 492682

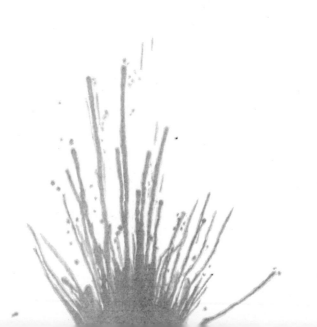

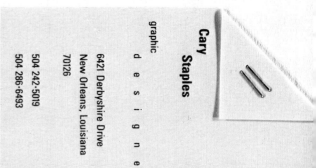

Cary
Staples

graphic
        d   e   s   i   g   n   e   r

6421 Derbyshire Drive
New Orleans, Louisiana
70126

Construtora
Abreu Machado Ltda

Construtora
Abreu Machado Ltda

Alameda dos Anapurus 1241   Indianópolis   São Paulo   SP   Fone 240 8102

SAM Repro as
Sagveien 11, Oslo 4

Telefon 02/35 49 57
Bank 1730.07.56506
Postgiro 2 06 84 68

Designers

Barbara P. Infranca, Bi Design, 16812 A Red Hill Avenue, Irvine, CA 92714

John Adams, Adams Advertising, 146 Donegall Dr., Toronto, Ontario Canada

Judy Eastwood, Advertising Center, Inc., 6213 Presidential Court, Suite A, Ft. Myers, FL 33907

Chris Galindo, Adwest Graphics, Inc., ·8380 Mira Mar Road, San Diego, CA 92126

Allan Niilo, Allan Niilo Illustration and Design, 2-2635 Granville St., Vancouver, B.C., Canada V6H 3H2

Chuck Nivens, Anna Macedo and Company, 469 Westmoreland Dr., Baton Rouge, LA 70806

Abraham J. Amuny, Art City, 16323 Craighurst, Houston, TX 77059

Gebriele Ugolini, Arturo UI, 47037 Rimini, Via M. Minghetti, 16

Cheri Moseley Groom, Atkins & Associates, 2455 N.E. Loop 410, San Antonio, TX 78217

Barry Zaid Graphic Design, 1515 10th St., Boulder, CO 80302

Gene Russell, Bay East Graphics, 171 Eastern Rd., Pasadena, MD 21122

Brian H. Crede, BC Graphics, 37 W. 20th St., Rm. 408, New York, NY 10011

Yael Dresdner, Beery Associates, Inc., 101 Fifth Ave., New York, NY 10003

Bruce Benke, Benke & Associates, Inc., 800 Roosevelt Rd., Bldg. C, Suite 4, Glen Ellyn, IL 60137

Linda Benveniste, Benveniste, 542 Broadway, 4-R, New York, NY 10012

Peter Birren, Birren Design Co., 502 Shadywood Lane, Elk Grove, IL 60007

Bob Calmer, Bob Calmer Photography, No. 1, 11th St., 11th & Cherry, Des Moines, IA 50309

Bob Costanza, Bob Costanza, 111-20 73rd Ave., Forest Hills, NY 11375

Bob Daniels, 265 Corona Ave., Suite D, Long Beach, CA 90803

Brenda Bodney, Bodney + Naranjo Design, 1216 W. Redwood, San Diego, CA 92103

Bruno Oldani, Designer, Bugdoy Alle 28 B, Oslo 2, Norway

Jeffery A. Yip, By Appointment Only, 3156 W. 19th Ave., Vancouver, B.C., Canada, V6L 1E7

Carol Banever, Carol Banever/ Graphic Design, 944 No. Martel Ave., Los Angeles, CA 90046

Carole Nervig/Dani Burke, Carole Nervig/Graphic Design, 1309 Spruce, Boulder, CO 80302

Wanda Greer/Denise Spaulding, David E. Carter Corp. Comm., Inc., PO Box 2500, Ashland, KY 41105

Cary Staples, Cary Staples Graphic Designer, 6421 Derbyshire Drive, New Orleans, LA 70126

Judith Harrison, CBS Entertainment, 51 W. 52nd St., New York, NY 10019

Judith Villarrubia, CBS Records, 51 West 52nd St., New York, NY 10019

Cheryl Lewin, Cheryl Lewin Design, 435 Park Ave., South, New York, NY 10016

Claudio Carvalho, Rua Dona Mariana, 205 Casa 1, Botafogo, Rio De Janeiro, 22280, Brasil

Claus F. Weidmuller, Polziner Str. 55B, 2000 Hamburg 73, West Germany

Clausen Advertising, 341 N. Maple Dr., Suite 410-A, Beverly Hills, CA 90210

Julie Gerblick, Communication Arts Inc., 1112 Pearl St., Boulder, CO 80302

Brad Copeland, Cooper-Copeland Inc., 1151 West Peachtree St., NW, Atlanta, GA 30309

Bob Cozad, Cozad & Associates, 15760 Ventura Blvd., No. 1803, Encino, CA 91436

Debbie McKinney, Crackerjack Studio, 5901 Peachtree Dunwoody Rd., NE, Atlanta, GA 30328

Mary Bogdan, Crayon Design, 415 Lemoyne, Suite 402, Montreal, Quebec, Canada

Raymond Nichols, Cypher + Nichols + Design, 503 Windsor Dr., Newark, DE 19711

Steve St. John, D' Acosta, 2108 Virginia Dr., Wichita Falls, TX 76309

Dalia Hartman, Dalia Hartman Designer, 2621 First Ave., No. 4, San Diego, CA 92103

Dan Reisinger, 5 Zlocisti Street, Tel Aviv, Israel

David Ayriss/Linda Holt Ayriss, 195 East Altadena Dr., Altadena, CA 91001

Davids Designs, 5, Riversdale Rd., Thames Ditton, Surrey KT7 OQL, England

Tracy Wilkinson, Design in Action, 14-16 Peterborough Road, London, SW6 3BN

Susan Feinstein, Design Office of Joseph Feigenbaum, 30 E. 37th St., New York, NY 10016

Ben Lai, Designers Express, 349 Lockhart Rd., 1st Fl., Wanchai, Hong Kong

Diane Moon Graphics, 504 N. Newport Blvd., Suite 202, Newport Beach, CA 92663

Laurie Schwartz, DYR — Art West, 4751 Wilshire Blvd., Suite 201, Los Angeles, CA 90010

Elaine Pantages, 7002 Boulevard East, Guttenberg, NJ 07093

Esteban M. Vallejo, Eve Creations, 9901 N.W. 80th Ave. (3-I), Hialeah Gardens, FL 33016

Cheryl Pellegrino, Fattal & Collins, 1119 Colorado Ave., Suite 104, Santa Monica, CA 90401

Felipe Taborda, Rua Barao Da Torr 274/401, Ipanema, 22411 Rio De Janeiro, RJ, Brazil

Nancy Stevenson, First Arts, 109 West 28th St., New York, NY 10001

Joe Shyllit, Fueha + Shyllit, 54 Berkeley St., Toronto, Ontario, Canada M5A 2W4

Medical Economics, Grady Olley, 680 Kinderkamack Rd., Oradell, NJ 07649

Toni Holzl, Grafik Design, Progettazione Grafica, Andrian/ Andriano (BZ), Bindergasse 2 Via Del Bottai

Garry Lay, Graphic Design Systems, 270 Esna Park Drive No. 12, Markham, Ontario, Canada, L3R 1H3

Robert Ebstein, Graphic Ink, 33 Commonwealth Road, Watertown, MA 02172

John P. Knutson, Graphics One, Rt. 7, Pine Point Road, Menomonie, WI 54751

Graphitecture, C/O Klair's, Cecil Court, 1st Fl., Bombay, India, 400039

Marnie Huckvale, Green & Huckvale Advertising Ltd., No. 1830-1055 W. Hastings St., Vancouver, B.C. V6E 2E0

Sandra Holt, Greg Newman Studio, Inc., 1356 Brampton Road, Pasadena, CA 91105

Hien Nguyen, 11948 Glen Alden Rd., Fairfax, VA 22030

George Pierson, Home Box Office, 1100 Avenue of the Americas, 4th Fl., New York, NY 10036

Patt Dietz, Hornall Anderson Design Works, 411 1st Ave., S., Suite 710, Seattle, WA 98104

Ian Price, 537 Wm. Kent Cresc., Manchester, M15 5DE, England

Images/1-4-16, 304 Azabudai Minato-Ku, Tokyo, Japan, 106

Jose Ortiz, J.L. Ortiz, 312 E. 93rd St., New York, NY 10128

Jack W. Davis, Jack Davis Graphics, 1826 Maynard Dr., Champaign, IL 61821

Jack Stone, Jack Stone Graphic Design, 1513 South Fourth St., Philadelphia, PA 19147

Jean L. Brady, 55 Fourth Place, Brooklyn, NY 11231

Jerry Cowart, Jerry Cowart Designers, 1111 S. Robertson Blvd., Los Angeles, CA 90035

Janice M. Lobbins, JML Design Studio, 1420 S. Michigan Ave., Chicago, IL 60605

Jack R. Anderson, John Hornall Design Works, 200 West Mercer, Suite 102, Seattle, WA 98119

John Oswald, Box 727, Station P, Toronto, Canada, M5S 2Z1

John Sposato, 43 E. 22nd St., New York, NY 10010

Jurgen Rieckhoff, Hans Henny Jahnn Weg 6, 2000 Hamburg 76, West Germany

Rose Farber, Kalur, Philips, Ross, 605 Third Ave., New York, NY 10158

Leslie Kameny, Kameny Communications, 928 Broadway, New York, NY 10010

Karen Fults Kaler, Karen Kaler Graphic Design, 13333 11th St., NE, Seattle, WA 98125

Ken Cato, Ken Cato Design Company, 74 Bridport St., Albert Park, Victoria 3206, Australia

Kristi Johnson Simkins, Kristi Johnson Simkins Design, 269 Columbus Ave., Tuckahoe, NY 10707

Mary Cunniff, Landor Associates, 46 East 61st St., New York, NY 10021

Michael Lee, Laurel Communications, 724 S. Central, No. 101, Medford, OR 97501

Clement Larosee, Legault Nolin Larosee Et Associates, Inc., 387, Rue St-Paul Quest, Bureau 204, Montreal, Quebec, Canada H2Y 2A7

Judy Moskowitz, Louis Nelson Associates, 80 University Place, New York, NY 10003

Melabee Miller, Louis Nelson Associates, 80 University Place New York, NY 10003

Marc Iso, Rua Barao De Masquita 510/104, Tijuca, 20540 Rio De Janeiro, RJ, Brazil

Marjorie Krasnick, 26725 Hendrie, Huntington Woods, MI 48070

Mark E. Lewis, 8330 Draper Ln., Silver Spring, MD 20910

Mark Lewis, Mark Lewis Design, 8330 Draper Lane, Silver Spring, MD 20910

Christie Macdermid, Market Design, 1275 Columbus Ave., San Francisco, CA 94133

Martha Voutas, Martha Voutas Productions, 1181 Broadway, New York, NY 10001

Nancy Secrist, Martha Voutas Productions, Inc., 1181 Broadway, New York, NY 10001

Melia L. Lyerly, 1015 East Blvd., Charlotte, NC 28203

Michael Levin, 36, Frishman St., 63 561 Tel Aviv, Israel

Michael M. Smit, 523 Manchester Road, Ballwin, MO 63011

Michael M. Smit, Michael M. Smith & Associates, 12935 N. Forty Dr., Suite 110, St. Louis, MO 63141

Michael Orr, Michael Orr + Associates, Inc., 75 West Market St., Corning, NY 14830

L. Chusu, Mike Berne Communications, Fook Hai Bldg., 150 South Bridge Rd., No. 13-01, Singapore, 0105

Mike Condon, Mike Condon, Inc., 1910 Ingersoll Ave., Des Moines, IA 50309

Mike Hodges, Mike Hodges Visual Communications, PO Box 390, University, MS 38677

Robert Midura, Mona Lisa Graphics, 388 Decator Ave., East Yaphank, NY 11967

Kathleen Conway, MW Advertising, Inc., 2029 Century Park East, No. 4390, Los Angeles, CA 90067

Ned Culic Design, 90 Clyde St., Kilda, Victoria, 3182, Australia

Norman P. Stromdahl, 4115 Broadway, Kansas City, MO 64111

Oswaldo Miranda (Miran), Rua Amazonas, 1207 Curitiba - Pr. 80.000, Brasil

Christine Owens, Owens/Lutter, 3080 Olcott, 200-C, Santa Clara, CA 95054

Ronald Kapaz, Oz Comunicacao Grafica, Dr. Homem De Melo 875, Perdizes 05007, San Paulo SP

Parsons Associates, 169 Cambria St., Stratford, Ontario, Canada N5A 1H6

Paul Davis, Paul Davis Studio, 14 East 4th St., New York, NY 10012

Paul Pullara, Paul Pullara Graphic Design, 10 Walnut St., Little Falls, NJ 07424

Peter Kerr Design Associates, Ltd., 89A Quicks Road, Wimbleton, London SW19 1EX, England

Peter Ravn, Peter Ravn Design, Strandgade 10-B, 1401 Copenhagen, Denmark

Pierre Drovin, Pierre Drovin Design, 7563 Drolet, Montreal, Quebec, Canada, H2R 2C6

Raul Del Rio, Portal, 21 Tamal Vista Blvd., Corte Madera, CA 94925

Larry Profancik, Priceweber, 2101 Production Dr., Louisville, KY 40299

Jean Alperton, Primo Angeli Graphics, 508 Fourth St., San Francisco, CA 94107

Lee Heidel, Provident Companies, Fountain Square, Chattanooga, TN 37402

Giorgio Davanzo, Publistudio, 30017 Lido Di Jesolo (Venezia), Italia, Via Mameli 93

Robert Cooney, R.A. Cooney, Inc., 50 East 50th St., New York, NY 10022

John Dudash, R. Falk Design Group, 4425 W. Pine, St. Louis, MO 63108

Michel Meyer, Radio Noisz Ensemble, IM Grundel 2, 6943, Birkenau

Richard Muller, Konkordia Str. 89, D-4000 Dusseldorf 1, West Germany

Richard J. Sawyer, Rick Sawyer, Inc., PO Box 308, Spring, TX 77383

Rinaldo Cutini Graphic Designer, 24 Via G. Favretto, 00147, Roma

Robert Anthony Casey & Associates, 725 Liberty Ave., Pittsburgh, PA 15222

Robert Minuzzo/William D. Gibbs, Industrial Center Bldg., Rm. 350, Sausalito, CA 94965

Rocco Anthony Russo, 360 East 55th St., New York, NY 10022

Ronny Shinder, Rough Layout, 46 Noble St., Studio 212, Toronto, Ontario, Canada, M6K 2C9

Shinzo Saiki, Saiki & Associates, Inc., 154 West 18th St., No. 2-D, New York, NY 10011

Beth Synder, Sales By Design/The Martin Agency, 1520 W. Main St., Richmond, VA 23220

James McDonald, Salthouse, Torre, Ferrante, Inc., 301 Rt. 17 North, Rutherford, NJ 07070

Sandy Blake, Sandy Blake, Illustration & Design, 645 Kittredge, Aurora, CO 80011

Scott H. Osborne, Scott H. Osborne Design, 51 Rockledge Rd., Apt 1-A, Hartsdale, NY 10530

Wayne Pederson, Seay Design Office, 2122 P St., NW, Washington, DC 20037

April Reeves, See Level Design, 5996 Crown St., Vancouver, B.C., V6N 2B8

Gerry Simons, Simons Group, 8770 Research Blvd., Suite 202, Austin, TX 78758

Susan Martz/Don Sparkman, Sparkman/Bartholomew Associates, 1144 18th St., NW, No. 300, Washington, DC 20036

Lori Stetson, Stetson Turner Associates, 101 South Warren St., Syracuse, NY 13202

Studio Krog, Krizevniska 9, 61000 Ljubljana, Yugoslavia

Cindy Slayton, Studiographix, 350 Phelps Ct., No. 310, Irving, TX 75038

Susan Mayer, 410 East 20th St., New York, NY 10009

Suzanne Anderson, Suzanne Anderson & Associates., 3355 Lenox Rd., Suite 200, Atlanta, GA 30326

Michael Waitsman, Systhesis Concepts, Inc., 612 N. Michigan Ave., Chicago, IL 60611

Roy Marshall, Tavernier, Perez, Kappler & Bitetto, Inc., 4401 W. Kennedy Blvd., Suite 300, Tampa, FL 33609

Laura Holman, Taylor & Wilson, 3440 Wilshire Blvd., No. 603, Los Angeles, CA 90010

Arne Ratermanis, Ted Hansen Design, 1955 Fourth Ave., San Diego, CA 92101

Naomie Sakanoue, The Adams Group, Inc., 100 Park Ave., Rockville, MD 20850

Barbara A. Pitfido/Rich Salzman, The Art House, Rt. 1, Box 158, Cadyville, NY 12918

Ark Stein, The Blank Design Group, 530 Lytton Ave., Palo Alto, CA 94301

Barbara Borejko, The Catalogue Group, 142 Fifth Ave., New York, NY 10011

The Creative Edge, 1514 San Ignacio, Suite 100, Coral Gables, FL 33146

Jim Wise/Valorie Danner, The Eye, 100 Colony Square, Suite, 2005, Atlanta, GA 30361

The Group Advertising Limited, 2A Kam Sing Mansion, 151 Jaffe Road, Wanchai, Hong Kong

Jim Allen, The Jim Allen Design Team Ltd., Thames Wharf, Rainville Road, London W6 9HA

Robynne Ranft, The Ranft Plan, 505 - 119 W. Pender, Vancouver, B.C., Canada, V6B 1S5

Janet Nebel, The Woods Group, Inc., 1502 Woodlawn Drive, Baltimore, MD 21207

Thomas Hillman, Thomas Hillman Design, 193 Middle St., Portland, ME 04101

Linda Wyman, Tim Girvin Design, Inc., 911 Western Ave., No. 408, Seattle, WA 98104

Tim Hanlon, Tim Hanlon Design, 7729 Lockheed, Suite B, El Paso, TX 79925

Arthur Beckenstein, Time, Inc., 1271 Ave. of the Americas, Rm. 3817, New York, NY 10020

Tony Agpoon, Tony Agpoon Design, 410 Townsend St., San Francisco, CA 94107

Wendy Chan, Tony Paris Associates, Inc., 137 East 25th St., New York, NY 10010

Bert Tanimoto, UMI Design, 2912 W. Compton Blvd., No. 204, Gardena, CA 90249

Gene Vitale, Vitale & Associates, 7104 Langston Drive, Austin, TX 78723

Belinda Von Feldt, Von Feldt Graphic Design, 670 Inca., Denver, CO 80204

Walter McCord, Jr., Walter R. McCord, 427 Club Lane, Louisville, KY 40207

Bob Warkulwiz, Warkulwiz Design Associates, 123 South 22nd St., Philadelphia, PA 19103

Scott McBride, Way Out West Graphic Design, 909 Sansome, San Francisco, CA 94111

Wendy Griffith, 29 S. 19th St., Philadelphia, PA 19103

Warren Wilkins, Wilkins & Peterson, 206 Third Ave., South, Seattle, WA 98104

Erica K. Wilson, Wilson & Wilson, 507 Granger Terrace, Suite 4, Sunnyvale, CA 94087

Xavier-Feal, Designer, 36, Rue De Picpus, 36, 75012 Paris, 1.3070546

Ed Young, Young & Martin Design, 550 Pharr Road, NE, Suite 340, Atlanta, GA 30305

TSI Communications, 16 West 46th Street, New York, NY 10016

ParaGraphics, 58 Haverford Street, Hamden, CT 06517